BRITAIN'S ETHNIC MINORITIES

The Policy Studies Institute (PSI) is Britain's leading independent research organisation undertaking studies of economic, industrial and social policy, and the workings of political institutions.

PSI is a registered charity, run on a non-profit basis, and is not associated with any political party, pressure group or commercial interest.

PSI attaches great importance to covering a wide range of subject areas with its multi-disciplinary approach. The Institute's 40+ researchers are organised in teams which currently cover the following programmes:

Family Finances – *Employment* – *Information Policy* – *Social Justice and Social Order* – *Health Studies and Social Care* – *Education* – *Industrial Policy and Futures* – *Arts and the Cultural Industries* – *Environment and Quality of Life*

This publication arises from the Employment Studies programme and is one of over 30 publications made available by the Institute each year.

Information about the work of PSI, and a catalogue of available books can be obtained from:

Marketing Department, PSI
100 Park Village East, London NW1 3SR

Britain's Ethnic Minorities

An analysis of the Labour Force Survey

Trevor Jones

Policy Studies Institute
London

The publishing imprint of the independent
POLICY STUDIES INSTITUTE
100 Park Village East, London NW1 3SR
Telephone: 071-387 2171 Fax: 071-388 0914

The views expressed in this Report are those of the author and not necessarily those of the Department of the Employment or any other Government organisation or department.

ISBN 0 85374 552 8

PSI Research Report 721

A CIP catalogue record of this book is available from the British Library.

1 2 3 4 5 6 7 8 9

PSI publications are available from
BEBC Distribution Ltd
P O Box 1496, Poole, Dorset, BH12 3YD

Books will normally be despatched within 24 hours. Cheques should be made payable to BEBC Distribution Ltd.

Credit card and telephone/fax orders may be placed on the following freephone numbers:

FREEPHONE: 0800 262260
FREEFAX: 0800 262266

Booktrade representation (UK & Eire):
Book Representation and Distribution Ltd (BRAD)
244a London Road, Hadleigh, Essex SS7 2DE

PSI subscriptions are available from PSI's subscription agent
Carfax Publishing Company Ltd
P O Box 25, Abingdon, Oxford OX14 3UE

Laserset by Policy Studies Institute
Printed in Great Britain by BPC Wheatons Ltd, Exeter

Preface and Acknowledgements

This report is the outome of a research project funded by the Employment Department, and carried out between March 1991 and July 1992. It is the latest in a series of reports from the Policy Studies Institute (PSI) and its predecessor, Political and Economic Planning (PEP) arising from programmes of research into the social and economic condition of Britain's ethnic minority populations. These studies have examined the extent and nature of racial disadvantage in the labour and housing markets, as well as analysing demographic characteristics in comparison with those of the white population. The present report aims to fill some of the gap left by the ageing of the last national survey of ethnic minorities carried out by PSI in 1982. The findings indicate that there are important and complex changes occurring in the condition of racial minorities in Britain.

Since the analysis on which the report is based was carried out, another source of information about ethnic minorities in Britain has become available. The 1991 Census included a question about ethnic origin, the first time such a question has been included in the Census of population. PSI is presently in the early stages of work on the fourth national survey of ethnic minorities, which will utilise the results from the 1991 Census as they become available. This purpose-built survey of ethnic minorities will provide more detailed information and a wider coverage of subjects than is available from the current sources. It will enable a more refined understanding of the changes that are occurring.

I would like to thank my colleagues at PSI for the help and support received during the course of this study. In particular, I am grateful to David Smith for his detailed comments on the drafts of the report, and to Bernard Casey for his advice and technical assistance with the computer analysis. I would also like to thank Steve McKay, Colin Brown, and Dennis Brooks for their valuable comments on the draft report.

The views expressed in the report are those of the author and do not necessarily reflect those of the Employment Department, or any other government organisation or department.

Contents

Tables

Notes on the tables

1.   The tables are for Great Britain (England, Scotland and Wales) only.

2.   Results are not given in cases where the weighted base is less than 20,000. Cells in which this applies contain a star (*).

3.   Column percentages may not add to exactly 100 due to rounding.

4.   A cell containing a zero means that the percentage was less than 0.5

5.   The unweighted sample sizes for the main table bases are given in Appendix 5.

1 Introduction

This is a report of a programme of research into the condition of Britain's ethnic minority population carried out by the Policy Studies Institute (PSI) between March 1991 and July 1992. The research was funded by the Employment Department, and focuses upon the position of the ethnic minority population in terms of demographic characteristics, employment, housing, and other aspects of their lives. All views expressed here are those of the author, and may not necessarily reflect those of the Employment Department.

Continuity and change in ethnic minority circumstances

There is a wide body of research which outlines developments in the circumstances of the ethnic minority populations of Great Britain. The PSI and its predecessor, Political and Economic Planning (PEP) have conducted three major programmes of research on the social and economic condition of Britain's racial minorities, in 1966-67, 1974-75 and 1982. These studies have examined the extent and causes of racial disadvantage in employment and housing, and made detailed comparisons with the white majority population.

The general conclusion from all previous research was that racial minorities as a whole had substantially lower living standards than white people. In employment, people of Afro-Caribbean and South Asian origin have historically been over-represented in lower-level and more poorly-paid jobs, even when qualification levels are taken into account. Partly because they tended to be working at low job levels, ethnic minorities were subject to consistently higher rates of unemployment than whites. However, earlier analyses showed that even when the effect of job level was controlled, some difference in unemployment rates remained. In housing, people from the ethnic minorities tended to be in the cheaper and lower-quality accommodation. People of Afro-Caribbean and South Asian origin have displayed substantially different patterns of tenure, both from the indigenous population and from each other.

Research in the 1960s showed that a great deal of racial disadvantage was the result of direct discrimination in the labour and housing markets.[1]

1

Such open and direct forms of discrimination were made unlawful by the Race Relations Act 1968. The 1970s research looked more generally at various aspects of the lives of racial minorities in Britain, and attempted to analyse discrimination as one of a number of inter-connected sources of disadvantage.[2] Direct discrimination was shown to be still a significant factor causing racial disadvantage. The research showed, in addition, how disadvantage can arise not only from conscious acts of racial discrimination, but also in a more indirect way from the structures and policies of key organisations. The Race Relations Act 1976 extended the law to cover indirect as well as direct discrimination. This was an attempt to deal with an important part of institutional discrimination: those policies and practices which are to the detriment of racial minorities although race is not the explicit criterion leading to inferior treatment.[3] Research in the early 1980s showed that despite some changes in the circumstances of racial minorities since the 1970s, their overall position was still one of substantial disadvantage compared to the white population.[4]

Thus, three decades after the first major waves of immigration from the Caribbean and Indian sub-continent, research on ethnic minorities in Britain still showed remarkable continuity with earlier patterns. It is to be expected that immigrants who have to adapt to life in a new and very different country will for a time face disadvantages and difficulties. Also, those factors which heavily constrained the opportunities of arriving immigrants, such as widespread and overt discrimination, job opportunities concentrated in certain localities and industries and at low grades, and the closure of the public housing system, may have set a pattern of life for ethnic minorities which continued long after the constraints themselves had eased. Against this, there is evidence of a strong dynamic among ethnic minority communities which is driving them to develop beyond the social and economic niche which they filled for the first 20 years. The clearest example is the drive towards educational achievement (see Chapter 3). As Britain's racial minority populations become long-established, with an increasing proportion born in the UK, there is a need to examine how far the differences between specific minorities and the white population are at last narrowing, or indeed, whether they are widening in some respects and for certain groups. It is particularly important to establish whether the novel political and economic conditions that developed over the 1980s have caused patterns of racial disadvantage to change.

Since the 1960s, British governments have been officially in favour of policies to promote equality of opportunity and the removal of racial discrimination. We have already referred to the anti-discrimination legislation which was passed in 1968 and 1976. At the same time, governments have consistently sought to limit the flow of immigrants into Britain. In 1962, the Commonwealth Immigrants Act introduced controls on immigration, which were further tightened by another Commonwealth Immigrants Act in 1968, which was rushed through Parliament to restrict the flow into Britain of East African Asians holding UK passports. The Immigration Act 1971 added further restrictions: to gain the right of abode in Britain, people generally needed to be Commonwealth citizens (or citizens of the UK and colonies), and also have some substantial connection with the UK (like having a parent born in the UK). The 1980s have seen further restrictions on immigration in the form of two pieces of legislation. The 1981 British Nationality Act means that a person born in the UK is not automatically a UK citizen, as would have been the case before the Act. To qualify for citizenship, the person must have a UK-born parent as well. The 1988 Immigration Act restricted the right to appeal in certain deportation cases, prevented 'second wives' of polygamous marriages entering the country to settle, and made overstaying leave in the UK a continuous criminal offence.

Purpose

The general aim of this report is to fill the gap left by the ageing of the *Black and White Britain* survey of 1982, by collecting in a single volume the best available information on the characteristics of the ethnic minority populations in comparison with those of the white population. In addition to this, there are a number of particular reasons why such a report is now necessary.

There have been a number of publications analysing results from the Labour Force Survey (LFS) with particular regard to ethnic minorities, notably in *Population Trends* and in the *Employment Gazette*. But to obtain a full grasp of all the available information it would be necessary to study a series of such articles along with a number of the annual LFS reports. To date there has been no single report which summarises the results of the LFS in respect of minority ethnic groups.

Another problem is that the technical difficulties involved in the analysis and presentation of a number of years' results from the LFS become even more complex when one tries to incorporate the earlier PSI findings, because of detailed differences in the definitions used and the way that statistics are presented. Because of such difficulties, a special research project is needed in order to utilise the LFS data on ethnic minorities to its full potential.

Whilst the 1982 PSI survey covered people with family origins in the West Indies or the Indian sub-continent, the LFS data will enable more detailed comparisons to be made between a larger number of ethnic groups. For example, where the sample sizes are large enough, we show separate results for people of Chinese and African origin.

Most previous studies of the position of ethnic minority people have covered England and Wales only. The size of the Scottish ethnic minority population has been steadily growing over recent years. A comparison of the 1971 and 1981 Census figures shows a 40 per cent increase in the number of people born in India, Pakistan, Bangladesh, Hong Kong or China living in Scotland.[5] The LFS data permits the first survey of England, Scotland and Wales combined.

Finally, the nature of the LFS data allows a more detailed analysis of the position of racial minorities than has previously been possible. In particular, it is possible to analyse changes in minority unemployment rates over the last five years, as well as examine factors such as mobility in and out of the labour market and between different kinds of job and industry, which provide a possible explanation for such changes.

The report does not contain a discussion of racial discrimination, but rather focuses on differences in circumstances between ethnic groups. The nature of the dataset permits analysis in some detail of these ethnic differences, and highlights some of the main areas of racial inequality. But the degree to which these inequalities are caused by racial discrimination is not within the scope of this study. For a discussion of this, the reader is referred to the substantial body of research which investigates the extent of racial discrimination and the extent to which it explains racial disadvantage.[6]

Method

The LFS sample numbers are grossed up to provide national estimates, but due to the small sample sizes for people from ethnic minority backgrounds it is preferable to base estimates on three-year averages. The main body of the analysis covers the circumstances of the various racial groups in the most recent period for which data are available, 1988-90. However, the results for 1984-86 are also used to show some key aspects of change over time. Together with information from the *Black and White Britain* survey, this permits a comparison between results centred on three years: 1982, 1985 and 1989. The analysis was carried out on the PSI computing system, using the Quanvert version of the LFS data. In addition to the secondary analysis of the LFS data, use was made of the analysis carried out on a number of other surveys, including a Department of Education and Science (DES) survey of 1980 graduates (1986), the Youth Cohort Study, and the survey of ethnic minorities in Scotland carried out for the Scottish Office by Social and Community Planning Research (SCPR) and published in 1991.

Sources of statistics on ethnic minorities

During the 1970s, the Office of Population Censuses and Surveys (OPCS) published annual estimates of the size of the population of New Commonwealth and Pakistani (NCWP) origin resident in Great Britain. These estimates were based on information from the 1971 Census about birthplace and parental birthplace. An allowance was made for white people born in NCWP countries by means of analysis of surnames for some countries of birth. The figure was then updated by estimates of natural increase (births minus deaths from registration statistics), and of net migration (from the International Passenger Survey). It is believed that this method gave a reasonably reliable estimate of changes in the total size of the NCWP population at the national level during the 1970s. Because the estimates were based on data classified by country of birth and citizenship, they would only remain reliable if the following held true.

1. The number of ethnic minority people born in Britain to British-born parents remained relatively small.
2. The bulk of the migration of ethnic minority people was accounted for by non-British citizens.

This was progressively less the case as the 1970s went on. In particular, there was a growing number of ethnic minority children born in Britain to parents who had themselves both been born in Britain.

The 1981 Census did not include a question about parental country of birth, and due to considerable opposition at the final Census test in 1979, did not include a direct question on ethnic origin either. Thus, the LFS was (during the 1980s) the most important provider of statistics as to the size and composition of the ethnic minority populations. This will cease to be the case when results from the 1991 Census become available. The 1981 Census did provide information on numbers of overseas-born by country of birth, and on households of which the head was overseas-born. In 1981, this still covered most British-born children of people born in NCWP countries (households headed by a person born in the NCWP were expected to cover 90 per cent of the total population of NCWP ethnic origin).[7] Thus, the 1981 Census information is, at the moment, the most reliable basis for estimating ethnic minority populations by county and metropolitan districts.

Sample surveys other than the Labour Force Survey
The General Household Survey (GHS) has included a classification of 'colour' (based on the interviewers' own assessment) since 1970, and since 1983 has included a direct question on ethnic origin. However, it is generally accepted that the sample size is too small to give anything other than a broad national estimate of the size of the ethnic minority population (25,000 people were interviewed in the 1984 GHS compared to 151,000 in the LFS). We have included some limited information about housing and ethnic minorities from the GHS in chapter 6. The National Dwelling and Housing Survey carried out in 1977-78 produced estimates of ethnicity which at the national level were comparable to those from other sources.

The Labour Force Survey and ethnic minorities
The LFS is a survey of households living at private addresses in the United Kingdom, carried out on behalf of the Employment Department by the Social Survey Division of the OPCS. The first LFS was in 1973 and took place every two years until 1983. From 1984 to 1991 the LFS was carried out annually and consisted of two elements. First, a quarterly interview survey of about 15,000 households conducted in Great Britain, and second, a 'boost' survey carried out in March-May consisting of interviews in about 45,000 households in Great Britain and over 4,000 households in Northern Ireland. LFS data are grossed up so that they become estimates for the general population (of people living in private households). The weighting factors compensate for varying response rates among different sections of the population, which lead, for example to an under-representation of people living alone and of female heads of household in the unweighted sample. In recent years the response rate overall has been between 80 per cent and 85 per cent. From 1992, the LFS was expanded and became a quarterly survey. In 1979, for the first time the LFS contained a question about ethnic origin, which was modified for the 1981 and subsequent surveys. It is a direct self-identification question about ethnic origin, and takes the following form: 'to which of these groups listed (on the card) do you consider you belong?'. The categories listed on the card are: white, West Indian or Guyanese, Indian, Pakistani, Bangladeshi, Chinese, African, Arab, Mixed Origin, and Other. People who describe themselves as being of Mixed or Other origin are asked to describe their ethnic group in more detail. This makes it possible to re-classify many of these answers into the main listed categories. In recent years, about 7,000 out of a total of about 150,000 respondents annually state that they belong to one of the ethnic minority populations. The sort of information about ethnic minorities contained in the LFS results is therefore conceptually different from the

information that was available during the 1970s (with the exception of the PEP/PSI surveys which used complex definitions based on a number of different questions and an interviewer's assessment). Before the LFS, data about the ethnic minority populations was based on a purely geographical classification, of country of birth (or parental country of birth). The LFS provides direct information about the ethnic origins of the population irrespective of country of birth.

It should be noted that the LFS is a general purpose survey not designed particularly with ethnic minorities in mind. For example, interviews are carried out in English by a standard fieldforce, although a high proportion of certain groups, such as Bangladeshis, speak little or no English.[8] It is likely, for this reason, that the LFS under-estimates the size of groups having poor English (especially Bangladeshis) and that the results are biased in favour of good English speakers, who are more likely to be successfully interviewed. Evidence in support of this view is set out in Appendix 1.

Comparison of LFS estimates with those based on other sources

We have mentioned four main sources of information about the size of the ethnic minority population in Britain; the population of NCWP updated from the 1971 Census, the 'coloured population' estimate from the General Household survey, information from the 1981 Census based on country of birth, and the LFS data about ethnic origin. Table 1.1 compares estimates from the four different sources for 1981.

In terms of total population, the estimates from the different sources are similar. The LFS gives estimates which are higher than the mid-year estimates of population of NCWP-origin based on the 1971 Census data. This is to be expected since the LFS includes people of ethnic minorities born to UK-born parents, and also people originating from outside the NCWP countries. In addition, as OPCS have shown, the inter-censal estimates of net migration after 1971 probably under-stated the true situation.[9] A comparison between the 1971-based figures and the 1981 Census data shows a shortfall in the former's estimate of the population aged below 10 years in 1981. This suggests that the estimates of net migration under-stated the number of children entering the UK over the decade. Nevertheless, despite the different methods used to obtain the four estimates, there is a general consistency between the final results in terms of total ethnic minority population. However, the old estimates do not now appear to have done as well at measuring the size of the different groups within the ethnic minority population. Table 1.2 compares 1981 LFS estimates for different racial groups with those derived from the 1971

Census. OPCS argue that the main problem is the reliance on birthplace data. For example, a significant number of UK-residents of Indian ethnic origin were born in East Africa. Similarly, there is an anomaly in the old estimates of the population of Chinese ethnic origin. A large proportion of these people were born outside the NCWP countries, and therefore not covered by the old estimates.

The LFS estimates of UK-born people of NCWP origin are lower, partly due to a higher degree of non-response to the ethnic question for children than for other age groups. Unlike the old estimates which classified ethnic origin of children according to country of birth of parents, the LFS data are based on the subjective view of respondents as to the ethnic origin of their children. Evidence from the LFS suggests that of children with one white parent and one parent of mixed ethnic origin, a large proportion are classified as white. These factors would also lower the LFS result for UK-born people of NCWP origin.

Definitions
The LFS data on ethnic origin were coded into over 30 categories; for example, as well as a 'Pakistani' category there were 'Pakistani/white mixed' and 'Pakistani-other' categories. In our analysis we regard all of those who chose a category with a named ethnic group first as belonging to that main ethnic group. The classification of ethnic origin used is shown in Appendix 2. In this report the term 'Afro-Caribbean' refers to people who described themselves as of West Indian/Guyanese ethnic origin. This definition differs from that used in the Youth Cohort Study of England and Wales, which groups Black Africans together with Afro-Caribbeans.[10] In the present analysis of the LFS Afro-Caribbean and African people are treated as distinct groups. Like previous PSI surveys, the 1982 PSI survey of racial minorities did not cover Black Africans, but the Afro-Caribbean group identified in the present analysis of the LFS can be compared with the 'West Indian' group identified in the 1982 PSI survey. Some previous studies have used the term 'Asian' to denote all people from the Indian sub-continent, but this would be confusing in the present study, which reports some separate results for people of Chinese origin, who are also Asian. Here we will use the term 'South Asian' when we wish to refer collectively to people with ethnic origins in the Indian sub-continent. The terms 'ethnic minority' and 'racial minority' are used interchangeably. The use of the terms 'Indian', 'Pakistani', and so on is merely intended to distinguish between different groups in the ethnic minority population (people whose families originally came from the countries in question) and is not meant to carry any implications about nationality or birthplace.

African Asians

A substantial proportion of the population in Britain of Indian ethnic origin came to this country from East Africa, in particular Uganda and Kenya. The *Black and White Britain* survey in 1982 showed results for African Asians as a separate ethnic group. African Asians were defined as people who were of South Asian origin (on the interviewer's assessment) and who were themselves born in Africa, whose parents were born in Africa, or who were resident in Africa prior to coming to Britain. There is no information in the LFS concerning country of residence prior to arrival in Britain, and so our definition of African Asians is based on country of birth and ethnic origin data. The category of African Asians used in this report includes people who meet the following conditions:

1 identified themselves as Indian, Pakistani or Bangladeshi

   AND EITHER

2 were themselves born in Eastern Africa,

   OR

3 lived in a family unit the head of which and/or his wife was/were born in Eastern Africa.

This definition misses some people who were classified as African Asians in the 1982 survey, namely South Asians not born in East Africa and living in a family of which neither the head nor the wife were born there, but who themselves lived there prior to arriving in the UK. However, the definition adopted is the best available from the questions asked in the LFS. According to the latest LFS data for 1988-90, the estimated population of African Asians on our definition is about 268,000. Of the people in the dataset who described themselves as of Indian origin in the LFS, 31 per cent were transferred to the African Asian group, and 4 per cent of the people described as Pakistani were likewise re-classified as African Asians. None of the Bangladeshis were in fact re-classified as African Asians.

Notes

1. W.W. Daniel, *Racial Discrimination in England*, Penguin Books, 1968.
2. D.J. Smith, *Racial Disadvantage in Britain*, Penguin Books, 1977.
3. In law, indirect discrimination occurs when a person applies any requirement or condition which, though applied equally to everybody, is such that a considerably smaller proportion of people of one racial group can comply with it than the proportion of other people – unless the requirement or condition can be shown to be justifiable irrespective of colour or race.

4. C. Brown, *Black and White Britain: The Third PSI Survey*, Gower/PSI, 1984.
5. Patten Smith, *Ethnic Minorities in Scotland*, Scottish Office, 1991.
6. Field experiments to test the extent of discrimination in real life situations were included in the programmes of research reported in Daniel 1968 and Smith 1977. Similar experiments were again carried out two years after the 1982 survey: see C. Brown and P. Gay, *Racial Discrimination: 17 Years After the Act*, PSI, 1985.
7. 'Sources of Statistics on Ethnic Minorities', *OPCS Monitor* 82/1, June 1982.
8. The 1982 survey (Brown, 1984) showed that 21 per cent of Asian men and 47 per cent of Asian women spoke English only slightly or not at all. Levels of literacy among the South Asian population (especially Bangladeshis) are still lower: see Adult Literacy and Basic Skills Unit, *A Nation's Neglect*, London, 1989.
9. 'Estimating the Size of the Ethnic Minority Population in the 1980s', in *Population Trends* 44, Summer 1986.
10. D. Drew and J. Gray, 'The Fifth-Year Examination Achievements of Black Young People in England and Wales', *Educational Research*, 32(3), 1990.

Table 1.1 Estimates relating to the ethnic minority population, 1981

Year	LFS (total non-white persons) 000s	%	GHS (coloured person)* %	Mid-year estimates[+] (population of NCWP++ origin) 000s	%	1981 Census: persons in households with an NCWP[++] born head of household 000s	%
1981	2,092	3.9	4.5	2,010	3.7	2,037	3.9

Source: *Population Trends*, Vol 44, p.25 (GB)

* Interviewer's assessment of colour.
+ Based on 1971 Census, updated by subsequent birth, deaths and net migration.
++ New Commonwealth and Pakistan, excluding Mediterranean Commonwealth; virtually all persons born in this area describe themselves as 'white' in the LFS.

Table 1.2 Estimates relating to the ethnic minority population, 1981

Ethnic group	All persons Mid-year estimate*	LFS[+]
West Indian or Guyanese	533	528
Indian	626	727
(of which, from East Africa)	(190)	(186)
Pakistani or Bangladeshi	367	336
African	108	80
Mixed	237	217
Other	138	204
(of which, Chinese)	..	(92)
Total	2,010	2,092

Source: *Population Trends*, Vol 44, p.27 (GB)

.. Not available.
* See footnotes to Table 1.1.
+ Including persons who did not state their country of birth.

2 The Ethnic Minority Population

Current population

Table 2.1 shows estimates of the total size of the different ethnic minority populations for 1981, and in each of the successive years 1984-1990. The individual year data display substantial fluctuations for certain groups, which illustrates the need to analyse information by three-year averages, and 1988-90 average figures are therefore also given.

In the period 1988-90, the total ethnic minority population in Great Britain was about 2.58 million, an increase of about 399 thousand (18 per cent) from 1981. Overall estimates of ethnic minority population sizes derived from the present analysis of the LFS are slightly different from OPCS estimates, because of detailed differences in the definitions of specific minority groups. As is shown in Appendix 2, we have included a number of mixed race people in the individual ethnic groups. OPCS have used narrower definitions of specific ethnic groups than ours.[1] This explains differences between the present estimates of population change since 1981, and those of OPCS.[2]

According to our estimates, the ethnic minority populations in 1988-90 accounted for about 4.7 per cent of the total population of Great Britain; 94.3 per cent said they were of white ethnic origin, while 0.9 per cent did not say which group they belonged to.[3] The largest ethnic minority population is that of people of Indian origin which makes up 22 per cent of the total ethnic minority population. The Afro-Caribbean population is the only minority population to have declined since 1981, while the Bangladeshi and African populations have shown the fastest growth.

Age and sex distribution

Table 2.2 shows that the ethnic minority population taken as a whole still has a much younger age structure than the indigenous population. For example, 34 per cent of the ethnic minority population are aged below 16 compared to 19 per cent of the white population. However, there are substantial differences in age structure between specific minority groups. The Pakistani and Bangladeshi populations have a very large proportion under 16: 45 per cent and 46 per cent respectively. The age structure of the

Afro-Caribbean population is more similar to that of whites, with comparable proportions in each age group before retirement age. Nearly a fifth of the white population are post-retirement age, compared to less than one in twenty of the ethnic minority population as a whole.

Table 2.3 shows the cumulative age distribution of the ethnic minority population compared with that of the whites. This shows clearly the young age profiles of the ethnic minorities, especially those of Pakistani and Bangladeshi origin. Among each of these groups, over half of the population are people aged below 20, compared to a quarter of white people. This proportion rises to 83 per cent for the under 40 age group, compared to 56 per cent of whites. The different age structures of the various ethnic groups in the population are underlined by a comparison of the average ages for each. The average age of the white population is 38 years, compared with 26 for the ethnic minority population as a whole. The highest average ages among the minorities are in the Indian population (30), and the Afro-Caribbean and Chinese populations (both 29). The average age of African Asians and Africans is 25, but the very young profile of the Pakistani and Bangladeshi populations is illustrated by their average age of 22.

Table 2.4 shows the sex distribution of the population by ethnic group. In the early years following the migration, ethnic minority populations showed a marked imbalance in favour of males, since men tended to pioneer the migration, while women and children tended to migrate later. By now, the Afro-Caribbean and African populations have reached a normal balance, with females slightly outnumbering males. The Pakistani and Bangladeshi populations are still unbalanced, with 111 and 113 males per hundred females respectively.

Place of birth
Of the ethnic minority population as a whole, 46 per cent were born in the British Isles, compared to 97 per cent of the white population (Table 2.5). Of the various racial minority groups, people of Afro-Caribbean (57 per cent), other/mixed (53 per cent), and Pakistani (50 per cent) origin were most likely to have been born in the British Isles. The Chinese population has the largest proportion born abroad, with 74 per cent coming into this category. Of these, the majority were born in NCWP countries with 26 per cent born in the 'rest of the world' which includes China. Only 32 per cent of the Bangladeshi and 34 per cent of the African Asian population were born in the British Isles.

For all ethnic groups, the younger the age group, the higher the proportion of people born in the British Isles. Of all ethnic minority children under 16, 87 per cent were born in the British Isles. Within this, Afro-Caribbean children under 16 are almost as likely as whites to have been born in the British Isles, 96 per cent of them falling into this category. This compares with the more recently-arrived Bangladeshi population, of whom 37 per cent of the under 16s were born outside the British Isles.

Year of entry into UK

Table 2.6 shows the majority of the ethnic minority population not born in the British Isles arrived in the UK after 1960, only 12 per cent arriving before this date. The longest established ethnic minority groups among those considered in this report is the Afro-Caribbeans. Of those Afro-Caribbeans who were born abroad and are now living in Britain, 36 per cent arrived during the 1950s, and a further 48 per cent during the 1960s. The 1970s saw the bulk of immigration of African Asians and people of Chinese origin. The table clearly shows that the most recently-arrived immigrant populations are those of Bangladeshi and African origin. Whereas immigration of people from other racial groups declined after 1980, the opposite occurred for these two groups. Of all people of Bangladeshi origin born abroad, nearly half arrived in the UK after 1980, and the same is true for 40 per cent of African people in the same category.

Regional patterns of residence

The LFS has limited use as a source of information about the size of the ethnic minority populations in local authority districts because of the sample size and design. The most widely used source of local data about ethnic minority populations is the 1981 Census, which included a question on country of birth, and birth registration data, which gives information about country of birth of parents. During the 1980s, the number of people living in a household headed by a NCWP-born person has been used as an estimate of ethnic minority populations in local areas. In the early 1980s most British-born children in ethnic minority groups were young enough to be still living in the households of overseas-born parents. But as time progresses, an increasing proportion of ethnic minority children are being born to British-born parents, and country of birth of parents is an increasingly inaccurate proxy for ethnic origin. Until the results of the 1991 Census become available, estimates of ethnic minority populations in local areas will necessarily be based on somewhat rough approximations. This is a particular problem in that there is a large demand for statistical information about the size of ethnic minority populations in local authority areas (mainly from local authorities themselves or related organisations).

John Haskey combines data from the LFS and the 1981 Census to obtain estimates of ethnic minority populations in county and metropolitan districts in England and Wales.[4] This method first uses 1981 LFS data to produce tables for country of birth by ethnic group, for each 'control area' (that is, each larger area for which the LFS can estimate ethnic minority population: see Table 2.7). The 1981 Census local authority population counts are then converted into counts by country of birth (COB) and ethnic group. This is done by applying the COB/ethnic group proportions for the control area of the local authority under consideration, and derived in the first stage from the LFS. This gives estimates for country of birth and ethnic group for each local authority area in 1981. The next step is to adjust for population growth or decline after 1981, using population change ratios derived for each control area by comparing LFS data for 1981 and 1986-88. After some other adjustments, for the 'not stated' country of birth and ethnic group figures in the LFS, Haskey was able to produce estimates of ethnic minority populations in each local authority district which are reasonable approximations for 1986-88. However, he stresses that this method is not reliable for estimating change over time, as the estimates of population change 1981-1986/88 for individual local authorities are not thought to be very accurate.

Thus, based on LFS-related updates of the 1981 Census figures, we are unable to say a great deal about changes in geographical concentration of the ethnic minority population at the local level. The LFS does give estimates of ethnic minority populations by metropolitan counties and 'regional remainders'. Table 2.7 shows the distribution for the three years 1988-90. The ethnic minority population as a whole is heavily concentrated in the South-East region, with 42 per cent living in the Greater London area compared to about 10 per cent of the white population. For each individual group within the ethnic minority population, the biggest single concentration is in the Greater London area. The Pakistani population is less concentrated in Greater London, and more evenly distributed between three other areas: 19 per cent of people of Pakistani origin live in Greater London, 19 per cent in the Yorkshire and Humberside region, 16 per cent in the West Midlands Metropolitan County, and 12 per cent in the Greater Manchester area. Nearly half of the Indian population live in the South East region, with 36 per cent in Greater London. However, nearly a fifth live in the West Midlands Metropolitan County. Whilst 55 per cent of the Afro-Caribbean population live in Greater London, 15 per cent of their population live in the West Midlands Metropolitan County. A high proportion of the African Asian population also live in the Greater London area (about 50 per cent), but also over a tenth live in each of the two

Midlands regions. Of the Bangladeshi population, 47 per cent live in Greater London, and a further 10 per cent in the West Midlands region. Of the Chinese, 42 per cent are in Greater London with 16 per cent in the rest of the South East and 9 per cent in the North West. A higher proportion of the Chinese live in Scotland than of any other minority population. The group with the highest proportion (69 per cent) in Greater London is people of African origin.

Mixed marriages
Previous research has found that mixed marriages or cohabiting relationships, with one white and one ethnic minority partner, are more common among Afro-Caribbeans than South Asians. It has also found that ethnic minority men were more likely than ethnic minority women to have a white partner. For example, the PEP 1974 survey showed that the proportion married to a white person was 8 per cent for West Indian men, 1 per cent for West Indian women, 5 per cent for Asian men, and 2 per cent for Asian women.[5] Christopher Bagley had earlier suggested two probable explanations of the fact that minority men are more likely than minority women to have a white marriage partner. First, the men have in the past outnumbered women within each of the minority groups, so a marriageable man would be more likely than a marriageable woman to look to the pool of available white potential partners. Secondly, in Bagley's words, 'men have traditionally been freer to explore new territory and new social relationships than women'.[6] These two factors also account for the similar pattern of inter-racial marriage in the northern part of the USA.

Table 2.8 shows the percentage of married and cohabiting family heads with a mixed union. Mixed marriages (taken to include cohabiting relationships) are far more common now than in 1974. As in 1974, they are more common among the Afro-Caribbean population than among South Asians. Of all married Afro-Caribbean family heads, 27 per cent are in a mixed marriage. Africans have a similarly high proportion of mixed marriages, with 24 per cent in this category. The Chinese have a somewhat lower proportion of married heads of family in mixed unions (11 per cent), but the ethnic minorities with the lowest incidence of mixed marriages are still the South Asians. This is particularly the case for African Asians, among whom only 3 per cent of married heads of family are in mixed marriages. This compares with 6, 7, and 9 per cent respectively of the Pakistani, Bangladeshi and Indian married family heads.

For most ethnic minority groups, it is still more common for a man than for a woman to be in a mixed union with a white person. People of Chinese origin are, however, a major exception. Of married Chinese women, 23 per cent are in a mixed union with a white person – more than twice the proportion of Chinese men. Pakistani and Bangladeshi women are the groups least likely to be in mixed marriages. Only about 1 per cent of married women from each of these groups is in a mixed union.

Household types and family structure

Table 2.9 shows the distribution of types of household between the various ethnic groups (households are here analysed according to the ethnic origin of the head of household). For white people, the most common type of household is that containing one small family (see footnotes to Table 2.9 for definitions of family structure), with 19 per cent of white households in this category. Afro-Caribbean, African Asian and African households are all relatively likely to contain a small family, each with nearer to 30 per cent of households in this category. South Asian households are the most likely to have large families. About half of all Bangladeshi and Pakistani households, and about a quarter of African Asian and Indian households contain large families, compared with just 6 per cent of white households. Only a small proportion of ethnic minority households consist of people aged over 60 (about 6 per cent), compared to over 30 per cent of white households. Table 2.10 shows that for all groups, the majority of household heads are male. The proportion of male household heads is highest in the South Asian groups, with about 90 per cent of households headed by a male, compared with 75 per cent for white households. Afro-Caribbean and African households have the highest proportion headed by women, with 36 per cent and 28 per cent respectively.

Each individual household may contain one or more family units. Table 2.11 shows that of all Afro-Caribbean family units, nearly a quarter are female lone parents. This is a much higher proportion than for other ethnic groups: 6 per cent of white family units are female lone-parent families, although family units of African people also have a relatively high proportion of female lone parents (16 per cent). Taking the 1982 PSI survey as a baseline, the proportion of female lone parents has risen from 3 per cent to 6 per cent among white people, and from 16 per cent to 23 per cent among Afro-Caribbeans.[7]

Table 2.12 shows the number of dependent children below the age of 16 in family units amongst the different ethnic groups in the population. Given the much younger age structure of the ethnic minority population as a whole, it is not surprising to find that whites have the highest proportion of family units with no dependent children under 16 (73 per cent of all family units). The Pakistani and Bangladeshi populations have the lowest proportion of families with no children under 16 (about 30 per cent in each case). South Asians on the whole are more likely to have larger families, particularly the Pakistani and Bangladeshi groups. Among Pakistani and Bangladeshi family units, 35 per cent in each case have three or more dependent children under 16 (compared to about 4 per cent of all white family units). The fact that South Asians tend to have larger families is shown by the average (mean) number of children under 16 per family. Whilst for white and Afro-Caribbean families this is similar (0.5 and 0.7 respectively), the average for Indian, Pakistani and Bangladeshi families is over 2.0 in each case.

Growth in the ethnic minority population

As the figures quoted earlier suggest, the fastest growing groups within the ethnic minority population are the Bangladeshis and the Africans, whereas the number of Afro-Caribbeans has actually declined since 1981. This would lead us to expect that the balance between the various groups within the ethnic minority population will continue to change over the 1990s.

The growth of the total ethnic minority population can be broken down into natural growth (births minus deaths) and net migration. Chris Shaw estimates the components of ethnic minority population growth over the period 1984-86 by using a combination of LFS data, registration of births and deaths, and information from the International Passenger Survey (IPS).[8] He points out the inadequacies of using LFS data alone as a basis of estimating components of growth; the LFS gives no direct estimates of numbers of births or deaths within the ethnic minority population, nor any information about emigration. However, data of this kind are available from registration records and the IPS, which use country of birth as a proxy for ethnic origin. Using ratios derived from the LFS, it is possible to convert data based on country of birth to data based on ethnic group. Shaw divides the ethnic minority population into broad sub-groups, and uses LFS data to estimate the number of women of child-bearing age in each of these groups. He goes on to estimate the proportion from each category born in the UK and in NCWP countries, since it is to be expected that these groups will have different fertility rates. Registration data shows that fertility rates of the more recently-arrived immigrant groups tend to be higher, because the rates may be higher in the country of origin and because families are reunited after a period of separation. These rates then fall towards those of the indigenous population. The total period fertility rates for NCWP-born women are available from the registration data, and Shaw assumes that the rates for UK-born ethnic minority women lie midway between this rate and that for all UK-born women. Adjusting for births to mothers born in the Rest of the World and for births of mixed parentage, Shaw is able to estimate

18

the total number of births to ethnic minority mothers in the 1984-86 period. Numbers of deaths are estimated in a similar way, and net migration is derived from the IPS. He concludes that two thirds of the annual increase in ethnic minority population in the period 1984-86 was a result of natural growth and one third to net migration.

The most recent LFS data (for 1988-90) show a continued increase in the proportion of UK-born ethnic minority women in the child-bearing age group (see Table 2.13). Using the same broad sub-groups as Shaw, we can see that by 1988-90, over half of the Afro-Caribbean and African women aged 15-44 were UK-born. In the 15-24 age-groups, UK-born women accounted for over 80 per cent of Afro-Caribbean and African women. It follows that births to UK-born women already form a large proportion of the total number of births in these ethnic groups. A smaller proportion (22 per cent) of South Asian women of child-bearing age were UK-born, but in the 15-19 group 66 per cent were UK-born. So as Shaw predicted, UK-born women account for an increasing proportion of total births to South Asian women.

The pattern of change

In the period 1988-90, the total ethnic minority population in Great Britain was about 2.58 million, an increase of 18 per cent from 1981. The ethnic minority population as a whole still has a much younger age structure than the white population: this is particularly marked among people of Pakistani and Bangladeshi origin, whereas among people of Afro-Caribbean origin the age structure is much closer to that of the white population. It should be noted that there are increasing proportions of certain minority ethnic groups in the pre-retirement (45-59/64) age group. This age group now contains about a fifth of the Afro-Caribbean and Indian populations, so that the next 20 years will see increasing numbers of retired people from these groups. The historic sex imbalance has now been corrected among the population of Afro-Caribbean and African origin, but there is still a considerable preponderance of males among South Asians, especially Pakistanis and Bangladeshis. A comparison with the 1982 figures shows that this situation is changing. In 1982, males constituted 57 per cent of the African Asian population, 58 per cent of the Pakistani population, and 59 per cent of the Bangladeshi population. By about 1989, the African Asian population was 51 per cent male, and the corresponding figures for the Pakistani and Bangladeshi populations were each 53 per cent. There has been a slight increase since 1982 in the proportion of the ethnic minority population born in the British Isles. Whereas in 1982, PSI found that about 43 per cent of the ethnic minority population came into this category, the

LFS shows that this has now risen to 46 per cent. The greatest increases in proportion who are British-born has occurred in the African Asian population (from 24 to 34 per cent), and the Pakistani population (from 42 to 50 per cent). There appears to have been little broad change since 1982 in the overall regional distribution of the ethnic minority populations, although the 1991 Census data will provide more detailed information about changes in geographical concentration over the last decade.

There has been a large increase in the incidence of mixed marriages, especially among Afro-Caribbeans: over a quarter of Afro-Caribbean married or cohabiting family heads are in a mixed union with a white person, compared to 15 per cent in 1982. Except in the case of people of Chinese origin, men are more likely to be in mixed marriages than women. As in 1982, mixed marriages are far less common in the South Asian population. The 1982 PSI survey found that only 4 per cent of South Asian married/cohabiting heads of household were in a mixed marriage. The LFS results for 1988-90 show that among married heads of families, Indians were the most likely of the South Asians to have a mixed union (9 per cent) but this was still much lower than for Afro-Caribbeans and Africans.[9]

There are marked differences between the household and family structures among South Asians and whites. These differences largely stem from the younger age structure of the South Asian population, and their relatively high fertility rates. Thus, comparatively few South Asian households consist of old people, whereas a comparatively large proportion consist of large families. The average number of dependent children is four times as high in South Asian as in white families. However, the present pattern is characteristic of a transitional stage. The age structure and age-specific fertility rates of the South Asian population can be expected to approximate towards the patterns shown by the white population.

Bangladeshis and Africans are the fastest-growing groups among the ethnic minority population, whereas the number of Afro-Caribbeans has actually declined since 1981. Among people of Afro-Caribbean and African origin, it is probable that the great majority of births are now to women born in the UK. Among South Asians, it is likely that the proportion of births that are to women born in the UK will reach 50 per cent in the next five years.

Notes
1. The source for the ethnic breakdown in the LFS 1981 is *Population Trends* 67, Spring 1992.
2. Additionally, the recent estimates of the *total* ethnic minority population size given by OPCS are somewhat larger than those

presented here. They estimate a total ethnic minority population of 2,624,000 compared to our lower estimate of 2,577,000. This difference is accounted for by slight differences between the data sets used by OPCS and by this study. The former had available final figures for the 1990 LFS, whereas this study uses the provisional figures for 1990. Also, our dataset includes about 50 thousand people (weighted figure) in the 'White' category who were coded in the OPCS dataset as 'other mixed origin'.

3. Work by OPCS on the General Household Survey has suggested that most of the people who do not give their ethnic origin are white: see J. Haskey, 'Ethnic Minority Populations Resident in Private Households: Estimates by County and Metropolitan District of England and Wales', *Population Trends* 63 Spring 1991.

4. J. Haskey, 'The Ethnic Minority Populations of Great Britain: Estimates by Ethnic Group and Country of Birth', *Population Trends* 60, Summer 1990.

5. D. J. Smith, *Racial Disadvantage in Britain*, Table A14, p.51.

6. C. Bagley, 'Interracial Marriage in Britain – Some Statistics', *New Community*, 1.4, Summer 1972.

7. This comparison is not totally accurate, since the 1982 estimates are based on households rather than family units, but this probably makes no difference in practice. For the 1982 estimates, see C. Brown, *Black and White Britain: The Third PSI Survey*, Table 17, p.49.

8. C. Shaw, 'Components of Growth in the Ethnic Minority Population', *Population Trends* 52, Summer 1988.

9. Again, this comparison is somewhat difficult because the figures vary so much depending on whether one takes individual or couples as the base. The 1982 figures quoted here are percentages of *all* married or cohabiting household heads in a mixed union with a white person.

Table 2.1 Population by ethnic group, 1981-90

Ethnic Group	%	Estimated Population (Thousands)										%	Population Change 1981-88/90	
	81	81	84	85	86	84-86 average	87	88	89	90	88-90 average	88-90 average	Thous-ands	%
White	-	51,000	50,895	51,222	51,202	51,106	51,573	51,632	51,595	51,847	51,691	-	+691	+1
Ethnic minority	100	2,092	2,361	2,376	2,516	2,418	2,484	2,613	2,503	2,614	2,577	100	+485	+23
Afro-Caribbean	25	528	573	581	559	571	512	505	532	474	504	20	-24	-5
African Asian	9*	192*	242	221	271	245	256	294	256	256	268	10	+76	(+40)*
Indian	26*	535*	583	494	550	542	548	567	537	584	563	23	+28	(+5)*
Pakistani	14	284	370	400	404	391	378	470	424	457	450	17	+166	+58
Bangladeshi	2	52	92	102	118	104	116	92	128	109	109	4	+57	+110
Chinese	4	92	109	122	113	115	126	136	134	136	135	5	+43	+47
African	4	80	135	118	111	121	138	138	166	171	158	6	+78	+98
Other/Mixed	16	330	253	333	390	325	411	411	326	428	388	15	+58	+18
Not stated	-	608	829	637	607	691	467	343	684	499	509	-	-	-

Source: 1981-90 Labour Force Surveys (GB)

* Derived from OPCS 1981 estimate of African Asian

Table 2.2   Age distribution by ethnic group, 1988-90

Percentages

	All origins	White	Total ethnic minority	Afro-Caribbean	African Asian	Indian	Pakistani	Bangla-deshi	Chinese	African	Other/Mixed
Under 16	20	19	34	28	33	29	45	46	26	34	39
16-24	14	14	17	19	15	17	17	20	16	16	16
25-44	29	29	31	28	41	29	26	21	42	37	32
45-59/64	19	19	14	20	10	18	11	13	13	12	9
Post-retirement	18	19	4	5	1	6	1	1	3	2	3

Source: 1988, 1989, 1990 Labour Force Surveys (GB)

Table 2.3   Cumulative distribution, by age and ethnic group, 1988-90

	All origins	White	Total ethnic minority	Afro-Caribbean	African Asian	Indian	Pakistani	Bangla-deshi	Chinese	African	Other/Mixed
Under 10	13	12	23	20	24	18	29	28	17	24	28
Under 20	26	25	42	34	38	37	54	56	33	40	46
Under 30	42	41	61	58	59	54	69	72	54	61	65
Under 40	56	55	77	71	83	69	83	83	76	79	81
Under 50	69	68	87	81	93	81	92	90	89	93	91
Under 60	79	79	95	92	98	92	98	97	96	97	96
(Mean age)	(37)	(38)	(26)	(29)	(25)	(30)	(22)	(22)	(29)	(25)	(24)

Source: 1988, 1989, 1990 Labour Force Surveys (GB)

Table 2.4   Sex distribution by ethnic group, 1988-90

Column Percentages

	All origins	White	Total ethnic minority	Afro-Caribbean	African Asian	Indian	Pakistani	Bangla-deshi	Chinese	African	Other/Mixed
Males	49	49	51	49	51	51	53	53	51	49	51
Females	51	51	49	51	49	49	47	47	49	51	49
Males per 100 females	95	95	104	98	105	103	111	113	105	96	104

Source: 1988, 1989, 1990 Labour Force Surveys (GB)

Table 2.5   Place of birth by ethnic group, 1988-90

Column Percentage

	All origins	White	Total ethnic minority	Afro-Caribbean	African Asian	Indian	Pakistani	Bangla-deshi	Chinese	African	Other/Mixed
All age groups											
British Isles	94	97	46	57	34	43	50	32	26	43	53
NCWP+ countries	3	1	46	42	65	54	49	67	48	45	17
Rest of world	2	2	7	1	1	2	1	1	26	11	28
Not stated/not known	1	0	1	1	0	1	1	0	1	1	2
Under 16											
British Isles	97	98	87	96	91	94	87	61	72	77	83
NCWP countries	1	0	9	2	8	6	12	37	12	14	3
Rest of World	2	1	3	1	0	0	0	1	15	8	12
Not stated/not known	0	1	1	1	0	0	1	1	0	1	2

Source: 1988, 1989, 1990 Labour Force Surveys (GB)

+   New Commonwealth and Pakistan

Table 2.6 Year of entry of ethnic minority population born outside UK, 1988-90

Column Percentages

	Total ethnic minority immigrants	Afro-Caribbean	African Asian	Indian	Pakistani	Bangla-deshi	Chinese	African	Other/Mixed
1950 or earlier	1	3	0	2	0	1	1	1	3
1951-1960	11	36	1	10	6	5	5	6	9
1961-1970	33	48	30	42	35	15	20	23	17
1971-1980	32	8	55	32	35	32	45	29	31
1981-1990	22	5	14	15	23	48	29	41	40

Source: 1988, 1989, 1990 Labour Force Surveys (GB)

Table 2.7   Usual region of residence by ethnic group, 1988-90

Column Percentages

	All origins	White	Total ethnic minority	Afro-Caribbean	African Asian	Indian	Pakistani	Bangla-deshi	Chinese	African	Other/Mixed
England	86	85	97	99	98	97	96	98	92	96	95
Northern Region	6	6	1	1	0	1	2	4	2	0	2
Tyne & Wear	2	2	1	0	0	1	1	4	2	0	1
Rest of Northern Region	3	4	1	0	0	1	1	0	1	0	1
Yorkshire & Humberside Region	9	9	8	4	5	7	19	7	6	3	6
South Yorkshire	2	2	1	1	0	1	2	0	1	1	1
West Yorkshire	4	4	6	3	3	5	17	5	3	1	3
Rest of Yorkshire & Humberside	3	3	1	0	2	2	1	3	2	1	1
East Midlands Region	7	7	6	5	12	9	4	3	6	2	4
East Anglia Region	4	4	2	2	2	1	2	3	2	4	3
South East Region	31	30	54	63	63	47	31	62	58	77	59
Inner London	4	4	20	33	8	10	6	40	19	52	21
Outer London	8	7	22	22	41	27	13	7	23	17	22
Rest of South East	19	19	12	8	14	11	11	14	16	8	15
South West Region	8	9	3	4	2	2	1	2	6	1	6
West Midlands Region	9	9	14	16	10	21	18	9	2	3	6
West Midlands Metropolitan County	5	4	12	15	9	19	16	9	2	2	4
Rest of West Midlands	5	5	2	1	1	2	2	1	0	1	2
North West Region	11	12	9	5	5	8	18	8	9	6	9
Greater Manchester	5	5	5	3	3	5	12	7	2	2	5
Merseyside	3	3	1	1	0	1	0	1	6	3	3
Rest of North West	4	4	2	1	2	3	6	0	2	1	2
Wales	5	5	1	1	1	1	1	1	3	1	2
Scotland	9	9	2	0	0	2	3	1	6	2	3
Central Clydeside Conurbation	3	3	1	0	1	1	2	1	2	2	1
Rest of Scotland	6	6	1	0	1	1	1	0	3	1	2

Source: 1988, 1989, 1990 Labour Force Surveys (GB)

Table 2.8   Mixed marriage family units, 1988-90

	Total ethnic minority	Afro-Caribbean	African Asian	Indian	Pakistani	Bangla-deshi	Chinese	African	Other/Mixed
Percentage of married or cohabiting males[1] with a white partner	15	27	3	9	6	7	11	24	39
Percentage of married or cohabiting females with a white partner	13	21	4	5	1	1	23	13	38

1   Based on heads of family unit

Source: 1988, 1989, 1990 Labour Force Surveys (GB)

Table 2.9   Type of household by ethnic group, 1988-90

Column Percentages

	All origins	White	Total ethnic minority	Afro-Caribbean	African Asian	Indian	Pakistani	Bangla-deshi	Chinese	African	Other/Mixed
One Adult Aged 16-59	9	9	13	22	5	7	4	6	15	22	15
Two Adults Aged 16-59	16	16	12	12	9	11	7	7	16	17	18
Small Family[1]	20	19	27	28	36	24	20	20	25	29	32
Large Family[2]	6	6	21	9	25	23	53	50	18	14	12
Large Adult Household[3]	17	17	20	19	24	28	14	17	21	13	15
2 Adults, 1 or 2 60+	16	17	3	5	1	4	1	0	2	2	3
One Adult Aged 60+	16	16	3	5	0	3	1	0	3	3	5

Source: 1988, 1989, 1990 Labour Force Surveys (GB)

1   One or two persons aged 16 or above and one or two persons under 16.
2   One or more persons aged 16 or above and three or more under 16; or, three or more persons aged 16 or above and two under 16.
3   Three or more persons aged 16 or above with 0 or 1 person under 16.

Table 2.10 Sex of head of household by ethnic group, 1988-90

Column Percentages

	All origins	White	Total ethnic minority	Afro-Caribbean	African Asian	Indian	Pakistani	Bangla-deshi	Chinese	African	Other/Mixed
Male head of household	76	75	80	64	95	87	90	92	91	72	78
Female head of household	24	25	20	36	5	13	10	8	9	28	22

Source: 1988, 1989, 1990 Labour Force Surveys (GB)

Table 2.11 Percentage of family units headed by female lone parent by ethnic group, 1988-90

Percentages

	All origins	White	Total ethnic minority	Afro-Caribbean	African Asian	Indian	Pakistani	Bangla-deshi	Chinese	African	Other/Mixed
Female lone parent	7	6	11	23	3	6	9	7	2	16	11

Source: 1988, 1989, 1990 Labour Force Surveys (GB)

Table 2.12 Number of dependent children aged under 16 per family unit by ethnic group, 1988-90

Column Percentages

	All origins	White	Total ethnic minority	Afro-Caribbean	African Asian	Indian	Pakistani	Bangla-deshi	Chinese	African	Other/Mixed
No dependent children aged under 16	72	73	50	58	42	53	30	31	58	55	46
1 dependent child	12	12	19	21	19	17	18	20	17	20	23
2 children	11	11	17	14	26	18	16	13	15	14	21
3 children	3	3	8	5	8	8	13	12	8	6	7
4 children	1	1	3	2	3	3	10	10	2	3	2
5 children	0	0	2	0	1	1	8	9	0	1	0
6 children	0	0	1	0	0	0	3	3	0	1	0
7 children	0	0	0	0	0	0	1	1	0	0	0
Mean no. of children per family unit	0.5	0.5	1.0	0.7	1.1	2.2	2.0	2.0	0.8	0.9	1.0

Source: 1988, 1989, 1990 Labour Force Surveys (GB)

Table 2.13 Percentage of ethnic minority women in child-bearing age group who are UK-born, 1988-90

Age Group	15-44	15-19	20-24	25-29	30-44
Ethnic Group					
Afro-Caribbean or African	53	89	84	60	17
South Asian	22	66	37	9	2
Other ethnic minority group	30	68	43	30	12

Source: 1988, 1989, 1990 Labour Force Surveys (GB)

3 Education and Training

It is likely that a part of the disadvantage faced by racial minorities in Britain is related to their education. Previous research has shown important differences in educational background between people from different racial groups.[1] This raises the question of how far differences in job levels and unemployment rates between ethnic groups are explained by differences in levels of qualification and experience. When migrants move from developing to developed countries, one might expect the average levels of education and training to be higher in the adopted country. It is important to examine the degree to which such initial disadvantage is being overcome or, conversely, is growing. For example, as an increasing proportion of Britain's ethnic minority population are UK-born and UK-educated, we might expect a narrowing of the gap in terms of educational achievement. On the other hand, there is the possibility of some ethnic minority groups becoming trapped in a vicious circle, in which social and material disadvantages both contribute to, and are partly attributable to, poorer educational performance than the indigenous population.

Another issue is the degree to which differences in types of education are perpetuated. The ethnic minority populations originated in countries with very different systems of education and training from that which has developed in Britain. Different systems place different emphases on post-school education, job-related training, and the relative importance of education for men and for women.

This chapter will address these issues by examining current learning, education and job-related training. The findings on qualification levels will be particularly relevant in the following chapters on employment and unemployment.

Current learning

There is a substantial body of evidence which shows that people of Afro-Caribbean and South Asian origin are much more likely to stay in education after school leaving age than are white people. For example, the Swann Report provided information about the destinations of school-leavers in 1981/82.[2] In five local education authority areas containing high

31

proportions of Afro-Caribbeans or South Asians, 33 per cent of South Asians and 28 per cent of Afro-Caribbeans were going on to a full-time course, compared to 17 per cent of other groups. Similarly, the 1982 PSI survey found that in the 16-19 age group, the proportion of South Asians continuing their education is twice that of whites, a finding which holds for both men and women.[3] Young Afro-Caribbean women were substantially more likely to continue their education than were young white women. Afro-Caribbean and white men in this age group had a similar likelihood of continuing their education after school-leaving age. More recently, analysis of the Youth Cohort Study[4] has suggested that this pattern still exists. In the year following O levels or CSEs, whilst about 4 out of 10 white people stayed in full-time education, this compared with 5 out of 10 Afro-Caribbeans and nearly 7 out of 10 South Asians. These proportions dropped over the following two years, but Afro-Caribbeans and South Asians remained substantially more likely to be in full-time education than young white people. Females were generally more likely to stay in education than were males, with the exception of the South Asian population.

These earlier findings were consistent in showing a stronger drive towards educational attainment among ethnic minority groups than among white people, although partly because the minorities had experienced some schooling difficulties, this had not yet been reflected in the proportions successfully completing tertiary education. The statistics for admissions to universities and polytechnics in 1989-90 for the first time provide an analysis by ethnic group.[5] South Asians now form a higher proportion of admissions to universities and polytechnics than they do of the population in the relevant age group, while Afro-Caribbeans form about the same proportion of admissions as of the population.

The LFS analysis confirms the pattern shown by these various other sources. Table 3.1 illustrates the proportion of each ethnic group still in full-time education for people in the 16-19 age group. A much higher proportion of ethnic minority people in this age group remain in full-time education (56 per cent) than is the case for the white population (37 per cent). Amongst the population of South Asian origin, men are generally more likely to remain in full-time education after 16 than are women, whereas the reverse is true of the white and Afro-Caribbean populations. Amongst men aged 16-19, there are substantial differences between the various minority ethnic groups. For example, Afro-Caribbeans in this age group have a similar proportion to whites remaining in full-time education. Young men of South Asian origin however, are substantially more likely to be in full-time education, 75 per cent of African Asians, 55 per cent of

Indians, and 64 per cent of Pakistanis coming into this category. For women in the 16-19 age group, South Asians are again the most likely to continue their education, although Afro-Caribbean women are also substantially more likely than whites to do so.

There is a great weight of evidence from previous research to show that young people from professional or managerial families are much more likely to stay in education after 16 than are those from manual families. We will see in the next chapter that certain racial groups have proportionally fewer in the higher job levels than others; in particular the Afro-Caribbean, Pakistani and Bangladeshi populations. This would lead us to expect a lower proportion of young people from these groups to continue education after 16. Accordingly, the finding of higher participation rates among ethnic minorities than among whites is particularly striking. Table 3.2 shows that even within socio-economic groups (defined by socio-economic group of head of household), young people of 16-19 from ethnic minority populations are more likely to be in full-time education than are whites. We analyse this for ethnic minorities as a whole, as the sample sizes for individual minority groups are very small (see Chapter 4 for a definition of the socio-economic categories used). In the manual categories, young ethnic minority people are almost twice as likely as young white people to continue in education after 16. The proportion of young ethnic minority people from the skilled manual category continuing their education is higher than that of young people from the top white category.

Young people from ethnic minority groups are more likely to stay on at school after age 16 than are whites (Table 3.3). Of all ethnic minority people 16-18, 41 per cent are still at school compared to 35 per cent of whites. People of Afro-Caribbean origin in this age group are less likely to be still at school, 30 per cent of them being in this category. However, a further 25 per cent of Afro-Caribbeans are in some other full-time education, which means that among 16-18 year olds Afro-Caribbeans are still more likely than whites to be in full-time education.

Thus, evidence from the LFS strongly confirms the conclusion that young ethnic minority people are substantially more likely than whites to continue their education after school-leaving age. This could be a reflection of two factors. In particular, a greater motivation towards self-improvement through educational achievement amongst ethnic minorities. The Youth Cohort Study analysis already referred to has produced strong evidence that young ethnic minority people are at least as positive about school as young white people. There is also evidence of strong family encouragement of young ethnic minority people to stay on in full-time education after age 16. The same authors constructed a model of the decision to stay on in post-compulsory education which included the following variables; ethnic origin, social class, gender, and parental education (whether or not either parent was a graduate) and single parent versus dual parent families. They found that after attainment had been taken into account, ethnic origin was the single most important variable in determining the probability of remaining in post-compulsory education. Another reason for the high participation rate in post-16 education could be the special difficulties faced by young ethnic minority people in the labour market which make it harder for them to obtain employment. We present findings in Chapter 5 showing how the generally higher unemployment rates amongst ethnic minorities when compared to whites are magnified in the younger age groups. The next section analyses whether this greater proportion of ethnic minority people in the education system is reflected in measures of educational attainment.

Highest qualification
Definitions
Other studies which have compared the qualification levels of different groups have encountered the problem of arriving at a satisfactory system of equivalences. The value of a qualification depends upon the circumstances in which it is assessed or needed, and it is particularly difficult to compare academic and vocational qualifications. In order to compare groups of people according to their qualification level it is necessary to construct some sort of hierarchy, but the choices made when constructing it will inevitably be to some extent arbitrary. Our system of equivalences follows that used in the LFS and is set out in Appendix 3.

Main findings
The PEP and PSI surveys have found substantial differences in the pattern of educational attainment between whites and ethnic minority populations, and between the minority populations themselves. In the 1974 survey the average educational level of Afro-Caribbean people was found to be substantially lower than that of white people in the same age groups. The distribution of qualifications amongst South Asian people was highly polarised, between a substantial group who had post-school qualifications, and a larger group who had received little education, many not ever having attended school at all. The pattern found by the 1982 survey was largely the same.

Given that proportionally more people from ethnic minority groups are still in full-time education and therefore likely to be in the process of gaining some qualification, we analysed qualification levels for those of working age who were not still studying. This gives a clearer picture of the distribution of qualifications.

Table 3.4 shows highest qualification for men and women of working age not at present studying. Since there is a major difference in educational background between men and women, it is best to consider them separately. If all ethnic groups are added together, men tend to be better qualified than women. White men tend to be better qualified than men from other ethnic groups, with the exception of those of African, African Asian and Other/ Mixed backgrounds. Of all white men of working age, 48 per cent reported that they were educated to A-level or equivalent, or higher. The comparable proportion is higher among African men (62 per cent); about the same among African Asian men (44 per cent); rather lower among Afro-Caribbean and among Indian men (38 per cent in each case); and much lower among Pakistani and Bangladeshi men (21 per cent and 12 per cent respectively). The high educational levels of African men are reflected in the fact that a fifth have a degree or equivalent, twice the proportion of white men and five times the proportion of Afro-Caribbean men in the same category. African Asian, Indian and Chinese men are more likely than whites to have a degree, with 16, 15 and 15 per cent respectively reporting that they were graduates compared to 10 per cent of white men.

Men are clearly more likely than women to have completed a trade apprenticeship, and white and Afro-Caribbean men more likely than those of other origins to be in this category. Eleven per cent of white men, and 10 per cent of Afro-Caribbean men have completed apprenticeships. Pakistani and Bangladeshi men are least likely to have completed apprenticeships, with under 2 per cent of each reporting that they have done so. This is because the migration from Pakistan and, especially, Bangladesh is still recent, so that a high proportion of men originating from these countries spent their formative years in a country without an apprenticeship system on the European model. Looking at school-level qualifications, Afro-Caribbean men display a comparable level of qualification to white men. The most poorly qualified men are those of Pakistani and Bangladeshi origin, of whom 52 and 61 per cent respectively have no formal qualifications. This is reflected in the proportion of men reporting that they have never received any education at all. Bangladeshi and Pakistani men are more likely than men of other origins to have never had any formal education. We will see in the next section that this is very strongly related to age group.

Within the female population of working age, Afro-Caribbean and African women, and women from the Other/Mixed group are the best qualified (over 30 per cent of each of these groups have A level or equivalent, or higher). Afro-Caribbean women are the least likely to have no formal qualifications at all; by contrast, a very high proportion of Pakistani and Bangladeshi women are unqualified. Of these two groups, 69 and 76 per cent respectively have no qualification, compared with 36 per cent of white women. Relatively high proportions of women from these two groups have not received any education at all. The numbers of white and Afro-Caribbean women reporting no formal education are negligible, but 8 per cent of Chinese women and 9 per cent of Indian women are in this category. However, there are substantially higher proportions of Pakistani and Bangladeshi women who never received schooling, with 27 and 22 per cent respectively reporting that this was the case. This is strongly related to age, as shown in the next section. Other studies have also found that relatively high proportions of South Asian and Chinese women have never received any formal education. The survey of ethnic minorities in Scotland carried out in 1988-89 found nearly a fifth of Pakistani women in this category, along with 15 and 16 per cent respectively of Indian and Chinese women.[6]

Analysis by age

Table 3.5 shows the distribution of highest qualification by ethnic group for all people 16-24 and not still studying. Within this age group, men tend to be better qualified than women, except that among people of Afro-Caribbean origin men and women are similarly qualified. Among both men and women, Indians and African Asians tend to be better-qualified than the white population in this age group. Young people of African Asian origin appear to be particularly well-qualified relative to other ethnic groups. For example, 17 and 10 per cent respectively of their men and women in this age group have a degree or equivalent qualification, a higher proportion than for any other ethnic group. In this age group, Afro-Caribbean men are rather less well-qualified than white men, although the difference is not large: Afro-Caribbean women have about the same level of qualification as white women. Pakistani and Bangladeshi men are still relatively poorly qualified in this age group, although looking at school qualifications (A-level and below), the disparity is much less than in other age groups. The qualifications of Pakistani and Bangladeshi women, even in the 16-24 age group, remain much lower than for white women. Under achievement in education amongst Bangladeshi young people was noted by a Home Affairs Committee report in 1986. The report noted that one of the main reasons for this was difficulties with the English language.[7]

Further information about the educational attainment of young ethnic minority and white people is available from the Youth Cohort Study (YCS). Direct comparisons cannot be made between the analyses of the YCS and the LFS, for two reasons. First, the YCS analysis uses a different definition of Afro-Caribbean people, and furthermore groups all South Asians together. We have already found large differences between the African Asians and Indians on one hand, and the Pakistanis and Bangladeshis on the other. Second, the YCS follows the progress of groups of young people in the years between age 16 and 19, whereas the LFS analysis shows the highest qualification among all people in the 16-24 age group. Despite these differences, it is worth reviewing the YCS results in the light of the present findings from the LFS. The analysis by Drew, Gray and Sime is based on the first three sweeps of the YCS: these took place at the end of the final year of compulsory education (around age 16) and at the end of the two subsequent years. Taking the latest data available (for the end of the second year following compulsory education) the proportion having four or more O levels or equivalent was 31 per cent for whites, 39 per cent for South Asians, and 18 per cent for Afro-Caribbeans. Thus, South Asians were ahead of whites, and Afro-Caribbeans well behind. The gap between Afro-Caribbeans and whites was considerably greater among males than among females.

South Asians were behind whites on this measure at the age of 16, but overtook them over the next two years, as a higher proportion continued their education and obtained further qualifications. Afro-Caribbeans, too, were further behind whites at the age of 16 than at the age of 18, and caught up slightly over this two-year period.

The proportion having one or more vocational qualifications at National Vocational Qualifications (NVQ) level 1 or 2 at the age of 18 was 28 per cent for whites, 27 per cent for South Asians, and 34 per cent for Afro-Caribbeans. Thus, a higher proportion of Afro-Caribbeans than of other groups had vocational qualifications, while a lower proportion had academic qualifications.

By contrast, the difference in level of qualifications between Afro-Caribbeans and the other groups shows up only very weakly in the LFS analysis. There are two probable reasons for this. First, Afro-Caribbeans are tending to catch up with whites after the end of compulsory schooling. The group identified in the LFS analysis – those aged 16-24 – is dominated by people older than those included in the first three sweeps of the YCS, so we might expect the gap between Afro-Caribbeans and whites to be smaller. Second, the classification of qualifications used in the LFS is cruder than that shown by the YCS analysis: it does not show the proportion with *four or more* O levels or equivalents, but the proportion whose highest qualification is *any* O levels or equivalent, and the proportion whose highest qualification is any A levels or equivalent, where the equivalents may be vocational. In short, the LFS analysis shows that young Afro-Caribbeans and whites have about the same level of qualifications where academic and vocational qualifications are rolled together into a single, crude, hierarchy: but the YCS analysis shows that the level of academic qualifications is higher among whites, whereas the level of vocational qualifications is higher among Afro-Caribbeans.

The YCS analysis also shows that patterns of participation vary among 16-19 year olds according to ethnic group. The most popular choice for white people who stay in full-time education is to take two or more A levels over a two year period. Afro-Caribbean students are the most likely group to take vocational qualifications or O levels in the year after age 16. Particularly large numbers of South Asians were taking O levels in the first year after 16 and moving on to take A levels the following year. Hence, by age 19, young ethnic minority people did not lack qualifications compared to their white counterparts, although the profile of these qualifications was somewhat different. Afro-Caribbeans were more likely to be channelled into vocational studies, perhaps because lower levels of attainment at age 16. Consequently, the YCS analysis suggests that a relatively small proportion of Afro-Caribbean young people have A levels. This apparently contrasts with the LFS results which show the same proportion of people in the 16-24 age range (26 per cent) to be qualified to A level *or equivalent* in both white and Afro-Caribbean populations. Again, this is probably because of the system of equivalences used in the LFS (see Appendix 2), which takes in vocational as well as academic qualifications, and because the picture of attainment shown by the YCS at age 19 was incomplete.

Table 3.6 shows the distribution for 25-44 year olds. For men, whites and Afro-Caribbeans show similar levels of qualification to white men up to and including A-level standard. Pakistani and Bangladeshi men are particularly poorly qualified at all levels relative to other groups. African, Chinese, African Asian and Indian men are all more likely than white men in this age group to have a degree. Higher proportions of all ethnic groups have no qualifications than in the 16-24 age group, with the highest proportions again being found amongst Pakistani and Bangladeshi men (of whom well over half in the 25-44 age range have no formal qualifications). For women in this age group, Afro-Caribbeans and Africans appear to be better qualified than women of other ethnic origins. Both groups have a relatively high proportion who have received higher education below degree level, which includes nursing qualifications. Very high proportions of Pakistani and Bangladeshi women in this age group have no qualifications at all (over 70 per cent of both groups, including about a quarter of all women of these origins who never went to school).

Table 3.7 shows the qualifications of people in the pre-retirement age group of 45-59/64. For men, the whites are the better qualified group overall, although a greater proportion of Indians and Africans are educated to degree level. It is more likely that men in this age group will have done a trade apprenticeship (compared to other age groups), although this is mainly confined to whites and Afro-Caribbeans. This age group has the highest proportion of non-qualified people, in particular for the Afro-Caribbean, Pakistani, Bangladeshi and Chinese male population. Of these groups, over half the men are unqualified compared to 34 per cent of whites. The highest proportion of non-qualified men is amongst the Bangladeshis of whom 70 per cent come into this category. Women in this age group are substantially less likely than younger women to hold qualifications. Afro-Caribbean and African women are better qualified than other women in this age group. High proportions of women from all ethnic groups have no qualification, the highest proportion being that of Pakistani women. Four fifths of Pakistani women aged 45-59 have no qualifications. A substantial number of Pakistani women in this age range had no schooling at all (57 per cent), and over a fifth of Indian and Chinese women also come into this category.

Where gained qualification
Earlier research devised ways of classifying qualifications gained outside the UK to counter the argument that such qualifications are worth less than British ones. The 1974 PSI survey included a schema which erred on the side of under-valuing non-British qualifications, so that any results showing disadvantage within qualification levels would be strengthened. In the present study, we analysed qualifications by where they were gained, based on whether the date a person finished full-time education was before or after the date of entry into the UK. We found that of all the ethnic minority people with qualifications, about 64 per cent gained their highest qualification in the UK; half of these people were UK-born (Table 3.8). People from the ethnic minorities at each level of qualification were generally more likely to have gained them in the UK. For example, of all ethnic minority people with a degree or higher qualification, 55 per cent gained them in the UK; of those with highest qualification of A-level or equivalent, 73 per cent gained them in the UK; of those whose highest qualification was O-level or equivalent, 80 per cent gained them in the UK. Among the minority ethnic groups, Afro-Caribbeans have the highest proportion – over three-quarters of those with any qualification – who qualified in the UK (Table 3.9). Qualified people of African origin are the least likely to have gained their highest qualification in the UK, with 53 per cent having done so.

It is not possible to devise the same schema within the LFS that was used in the 1974 research. But we are able to compare unemployment rates and job levels of ethnic minority people qualified in the UK, with those who qualified abroad (for this analysis, see Chapters 4 and 5).

Job-related training

Table 3.10 shows that, of all dependent employees of working age (excluding those on government schemes), the same proportion of white and ethnic minority people reported that they had received some job-related training in the previous four weeks (13 per cent). Employees of African and Afro-Caribbean origin had a slightly higher than average proportion of people reporting some training in the last four weeks.

For men, again a similar proportion of employees from the white and ethnic minority groups reported that they received some job-related training (13 and 12 per cent respectively). Fewer of the Indian, Pakistani and Bangladeshi groups had received recent training, and more of the African and Other/Mixed groups, 19 and 22 per cent respectively. For women, the groups with the highest proportion of people reporting some job-related training in recent weeks were the Afro-Caribbean, African and Other/mixed groups, all with 17 per cent of employees in this category (compared to 14 per cent of whites). One fifth of all Afro-Caribbean women employees who said they had received some job-related training were nurses, compared to about a tenth of white women. People in all ethnic groups from the younger age bands were more likely to have received some recent training. In the 16-24 age bands over a fifth of male employees in all ethnic groups received some training, with slightly more of the racial minority groups than the white reporting training. This falls to figures of 7 per cent for white and 5 per cent for ethnic minorities in the 45-64 age band.

Training is more likely to be offered to those people working in the higher job levels, and table 3.11 shows the proportion of dependent employees who said they had received job-related training in the last four weeks, within job levels (for definitions, see chapter 4). In general, the above pattern is repeated within job levels: Afro-Caribbeans are more likely to receive some job-related training than whites and South Asians relatively less likely. In the professional, managerial, and employer category, Afro-Caribbeans were relatively more likely than employees of other origins to have received training. Of Afro-Caribbean male employees in the top category, 29 per cent said they had received some training in the last four weeks, compared to 19 per cent of white male employees. South Asian employees in this group had a lower likelihood of having received some training. In the other non-manual category, Pakistani male employees were relatively more likely to report receiving some training, with 30 per cent doing so compared to 21 per cent of whites. Within the skilled manual category, Afro-Caribbean and white male employees had similar probabilities of having received some training, with 11 and 10 per cent respectively reporting that they had done so. South Asians were slightly less likely to have received training. Smaller proportions again of the semi-skilled and unskilled categories reported that they received training, but a similar pattern is apparent with somewhat higher proportions of the white and Afro-Caribbean employees than of the South Asian employees reporting that they received some training.

In general, female employees in all job levels and from all ethnic origins were less likely than males to report job-related training in the last four weeks. The exception to this was in the top category, in which women employees were noticeably more likely than men to have had some recent training. Afro-Caribbean women in this group were the most likely to have received some recent job-related training, with 30 per cent reporting that they had done so compared to 26 per cent of white, and 25 per cent of Indian female employees. At lower job levels, smaller proportions of female employees reported that they had received some training in the last four weeks, with little disparity between ethnic groups. In all job levels, Afro-Caribbean women were relatively more likely than women of other ethnic origins to report some recent job-related training.

The pattern of change
There is strong evidence that young ethnic minority people are substantially more likely than young white people to continue their education after the age of 16. Very high proportions of young people from the South Asian groups stay in full time education after school leaving age. These findings are particularly striking because we would expect people from professional households to be more likely to continue their education, and these people form a smaller proportion of ethnic minorities than of white people. However, the relationship between social class and continuing education is far weaker among young ethnic minority people than among the white population. Young people from all ethnic minority groups are more likely than whites to continue their education after the age of 16; but Afro-Caribbeans are more likely than other groups to leave school at 16 and continue full time education in some other institution. A comparison with the figures from the 1982 PSI survey shows that in all ethnic groups, more people in the 16-19 age group are staying in full-time education. Whereas in 1982, a quarter of white males in this age group were still studying full-time, this figure has now risen to 36 per cent. The corresponding figures

for white females are 24 per cent (1982) and 38 per cent (1988-90). However, the increase in the proportion of Afro-Caribbean young people staying in education has been greater, from 26 to 39 per cent for males, and from 37 to 48 per cent for females. Although we only have the 1982 figures for all South Asians, Table 3A suggests that there has been a slight increase in the proportion staying in full-time education in these groups, although from a much higher base.

Table 3A   Percentage of 16-19 year olds in full-time education, 1982 and 1988-90

Ethnic group	1982 PSI Survey		1988-90 LFS	
	Men	Women	Men	Women
White	25	24	36	38
Afro-Caribbean	26	37	39	48
South Asian	58	51	60	53

We have found evidence that this much greater propensity to continue formal education is being reflected in a narrowing of the gap in levels of educational attainment between white and ethnic minority people. Direct comparison with the 1982 survey findings on qualification are not possible as they separated academic and vocational qualifications, whereas the LFS employed a system of equivalences (see Appendix 3). However, the general pattern outlined in 1982 was that Afro-Caribbean and South Asian people were less likely than whites to have formal qualifications. The findings from the LFS suggest that this is gradually changing, with the youngest age group of 16-24 better qualified than older generations. We would expect qualifications to be related to age group. Since the Second World War, there has been a general widening of educational opportunities, reflected in the above findings that each successive generation is better-qualified than the last. But the interesting finding is that young people are not only better-qualified relative to their elders, but that the disparity between white and minority groups appears to be less in the younger age groups. This is particularly apparent in the case of women. It is also clear that a gap is opening up within the minority population, between relatively well-qualified African Asians and Indians, and poorly-qualified Pakistanis and Bangladeshis.

The above results also illustrate cultural differences between different education systems. At the level of school leaving qualifications,

Afro-Caribbean people have a similar profile to whites; but the proportion with higher education qualifications is lower among Afro-Caribbean men than among whites, African Asians and Indians. Of the ethnic minority populations, the Afro-Caribbeans have the highest proportion who have completed trade apprenticeships. This partly reflects the education system in the West Indies which followed traditional schooling to age 15 with a well-developed apprenticeship system, but little higher education in the British sense. In the Indian system, higher education is more developed, trade apprenticeships are rare or non-existent, and there has traditionally been a large proportion of people receiving little or no education. Consequently, Indian people are generally either well-qualified or not at all, and very small proportions have completed trade apprenticeships. Similarly, education was traditionally seen as far more important for men than for women. Hence, a high proportion of older women originating from the Indian sub-continent have never received any education; this is particularly marked among women originating from Pakistan and Bangladesh.

The proportion currently receiving job-related training is broadly similar among white people and those belonging to ethnic minorities, although there are some small differences in detail when men and women, and people at different job levels, are considered separately.

Notes

1. The relevant research findings are summarised in D. J. Smith and S. Tomlinson, *The School Effect: A Study of Multi-Racial Comprehensives*, PSI 1989.
2. Department of Education and Science, *Education For All: The Report of a Committee of Inquiry into the Education of Children from Ethnic Minority Groups*, Cmnd 9453, London: HMSO, 1985.
3. C. Brown, *Black and White Britain: The Third PSI Survey*, Table 78, p.149.
4. David Drew, John Gray and Nicholas Sime, *Against the Odds: the Education and Labour Market Experiences of Black Young People*, Youth Cohort Study: England and Wales: Department of Employment, 1992.
5. Polytechnics Central Admissions System, *Statistical Supplement 1989-90*; Universities Central Council on Admissions, *Statistical Supplement to the Twenty-eighth Report 1989-90*.
6. Patten Smith, *Ethnic Minorities in Scotland*, Scottish Office, Central Research Unit Papers, 1991.
7. House of Commons, Home Affairs Committee, First Report Session 1986-87, *Bangladeshis in Britain*.

Table 3.1 Percentage of 16-19 year olds currently in full-time education by ethnic group, 1988-90

	All	Male	Female
All origins	39	38	40
White	37	36	38
Total ethnic minority	56	56	56
Afro-Caribbean	43	39	48
African Asian	66	75	56
Indian	58	55	61
Pakistani	55	64	45
Bangladeshi	46	41	*
Chinese	77	*	*
African	71	*	*
Other/mixed	58	55	62

Source: 1988, 1989, 1990 Labour Force Surveys (GB)

*   Sample size too small

Table 3.2   Percentage currently in full-time education by ethnic group and social class, 16-19 year olds, 1988-90

Social class of head of family	Professional/Managerial/ Employer			Other Non-manual			Skilled Manual			Semi/Unskilled		
	All	White	Ethnic minority	All	White	Ethnic minority	All	White	Ethnic minority	All	White	Ethnic minority
% in full time education (all aged 16-19)	55	55	69	45	45	62	31	30	59	27	25	47

Source: 1988, 1989, 1990 Labour Force Surveys (GB)

Table 3.3   Percentage of 16-18 year olds still at school or in some other full-time education by ethnic group, 1988-90

	All origins	White	Total ethnic minority	Afro-Caribbean	African Asian	Indian	Pakistani	Bangla-deshi	Chinese	African	Other/Mixed
Percentage still at school	35	30	41	30	46	45	38	45	*	47	42
Percentage still in full-time education	12	11	24	25	22	24	26	8	*	32	22

Source: 1988, 1989, 1990 Labour Force Surveys (GB)

* Sample size too small

Table 3.4 Highest qualification by ethnic group, all persons of working age, 1988-90

Column Percentages

	All origins	White	Total ethnic minority	Afro-Caribbean	African Asian	Indian	Pakistani	Bangla-deshi	Chinese	African	Other/Mixed
All Persons (16-59/64)											
GCE A level/equivalent or higher	38	38	31	35	34	31	14	10	33	50	41
Of which: Degree/equivalent	8	8	9	3	13	12	4	6	13	14	16
Higher education below degree level	6	6	6	8	4	4	1	1	10	13	7
GCE A level/equivalent	24	24	16	24	17	14	9	4	11	24	18
Of which: BTEC(general)/ONC/OND	2	2	2	3	3	2	1	0	1	6	3
City & Guilds	9	9	5	10	4	3	2	0	1	7	5
GCE A level or equivalent	6	6	6	5	7	6	4	2	6	8	8
Trade apprenticeship	7	7	3	6	3	2	1	1	2	3	3
GCE O level/equivalent	17	17	13	16	17	11	8	8	9	19	15
CSE (not grade 1)	5	5	5	9	5	4	3	4	1	2	4
Other	7	7	11	5	14	12	11	10	10	11	16
None	32	32	38	33	29	39	60	68	44	17	23
(Never received any education)	0	0	6	1	1	6	18	15	7	2	1
Not stated/not known	1	1	2	2	2	3	3	1	2	2	1

Contd

Table 3.4 Highest qualification by ethnic group, all persons of working age, 1988-90 (contd)

Column Percentages

	All origins	White	Total ethnic minority	Afro-Caribbean	African Asian	Indian	Pakistani	Bangla-deshi	Chinese	African	Other/Mixed
Men (16-64)											
GCE A level/equivalent or higher	48	48	38	38	44	38	21	12	34	62	48
Of which: Degree/equivalent	10	10	12	4	16	15	5	7	15	20	19
Higher education below degree level	5	5	4	2	5	4	2	0	3	10	5
GCE A level/equivalent	33	33	22	31	23	19	13	5	15	32	24
Of which: BTEC(general)/ONC/OND	3	3	3	3	3	3	1	0	3	9	3
City & Guilds	14	14	7	14	5	5	4	1	2	8	8
A level or equivalent	5	5	7	4	10	7	6	3	8	12	8
Trade apprenticeship	10	11	5	10	5	4	2	1	4	3	4
GCE O level/equivalent	12	12	11	12	14	9	8	8	10	14	13
CSE (not grade 1)	4	4	4	7	3	3	3	6	2	1	4
Other	7	6	11	6	14	12	12	12	10	8	14
None	28	28	34	35	23	34	52	61	42	13	19
(Never received any education)	0	0	3	1	1	4	8	9	5	0	1
Not stated/not known	1	1	3	2	2	4	4	1	3	3	2

Contd

Table 3.4 Highest qualification by ethnic group, all persons of working age, 1988-90 (contd)

Column Percentages

	All origins	White	Total ethnic minority	Afro-Caribbean	African Asian	Indian	Pakistani	Bangla-deshi	Chinese	African	Other/Mixed
Women (16-59)											
GCE A level/equivalent or higher	27	27	25	32	23	23	8	7	31	38	34
Of which: Degree/equivalent	6	6	7	3	9	9	3	4	10	7	12
Higher education below degree level	7	7	8	13	3	5	1	1	15	15	9
GCE A level/equivalent	14	14	11	16	11	9	4	2	6	15	13
Of which: BTEC (general)/ONC/OND	2	2	2	2	3	2	1	0	0	3	3
City & Guilds	4	4	2	5	2	1	0	0	1	5	2
GCE A level or equivalent	6	6	5	6	5	6	3	2	4	5	7
Trade apprenticeship	2	2	1	2	0	0	0	0	1	2	2
GCE O level/equivalent	22	22	15	19	20	14	8	8	9	24	17
CSE (not grade 1)	6	6	6	11	6	5	3	2	1	2	5
Other	8	8	11	5	14	11	10	7	10	14	17
None	36	36	42	31	35	45	69	76	46	22	27
(Never received any education)	0	0	8	0	2	9	27	22	8	4	1
Noted stated/not known	1	1	1	1	2	1	2	1	2	1	0

Source: 1988, 1989, 1990 Labour Force Surveys (GB)

Table 3.5 Highest qualification by ethnic group, 16-24 age group, 1988-90

Column Percentages

	All origins	White	Total ethnic minority	Afro-Caribbean	African Asian	Indian	Pakistani	Bangla-deshi	Chinese	African	Other/Mixed
All Persons (16-24)											
GCE A level/equivalent or higher	33	33	30	30	41	36	18	5	44	40	28
Of which: Degree/equivalent	4	4	5	1	13	6	2	2	12	5	7
Higher education below degree level	3	3	2	2	2	3	1	0	9	4	3
GCE A level/equivalent	26	26	22	26	26	27	15	3	24	30	18
Of which: BTEC (general)/ONC/OND	5	5	6	5	7	7	4	0	6	16	5
City & Guilds	10	10	7	12	7	8	4	0	4	7	4
GCE A level or equivalent	9	9	9	8	11	12	7	3	13	6	9
Trade apprenticeship	2	3	1	1	1	1	0	0	0	1	0
GCE O level/equivalent	30	30	25	28	20	25	18	16	31	30	31
CSE (not grade 1)	13	13	12	17	14	10	9	13	3	3	13
Other	3	3	5	3	7	5	5	10	5	8	6
None	21	20	27	21	18	22	48	54	15	7	20
(Never received any education)	0	0	2	0	1	0	8	5	0	2	0
Not stated/not known	1	1	2	2	0	2	3	1	2	2	2

Contd

Table 3.5 Highest qualification by ethnic group, 16-24 age group, 1988-90 (contd)

Column Percentages

	All origins	White	Total ethnic minority	Afro-Caribbean	African Asian	Indian	Pakistani	Bangla-deshi	Chinese	African	Other/Mixed
Men (16-24)											
GCE A level/equivalent or higher	37	37	34	30	49	41	25	7	*	54	28
Of which: Degree/equivalent	4	4	5	0	17	7	3	2	*	6	7
Higher education below degree level	3	3	2	1	3	3	1	0	*	5	1
GCE A level/equivalent	30	30	26	28	28	32	22	5	*	43	19
Of which: BTEC(general)/ONC/OND	5	5	7	6	7	8	4	0	*	25	2
City & Guilds	14	14	9	13	6	9	8	0	*	10	6
GCE A level or equivalent	8	8	10	7	15	13	9	5	*	9	10
Trade apprenticeship	3	3	1	2	0	1	0	0	*	0	1
GCE O level/equivalent	24	24	24	24	19	22	23	18	*	20	35
CSE (not grade 1)	13	13	12	16	16	9	8	19	*	5	14
Other	3	2	4	4	3	3	4	11	*	4	4
None	22	22	24	26	13	22	34	45	*	14	17
(Never received any education)	0	0	1	0	0	0	1	4	*	0	0
Not stated/not known	1	1	2	1	0	2	5	0	3	3	3

Contd

Table 3.5   Highest qualification by ethnic group, 16-24 age group, 1988-90 (contd)

Column Percentages

	All origins	White	Total ethnic minority	Afro-Caribbean	African Asian	Indian	Pakistani	Bangla-deshi	Chinese	African	Other/Mixed
Women (16-24)											
GCE A level/equivalent or higher	29	29	26	30	36	31	12	4	*	25	28
Of which: Degree/equivalent	3	3	4	2	10	5	2	2	*	4	7
Higher education below degree level	3	3	3	3	2	4	1	0	*	4	4
GCE A level/equivalent	22	22	19	24	25	23	9	2	*	16	17
Of which: BTEC(general)/ONC/OND	4	4	5	4	7	6	3	0	*	7	8
City & Guilds	7	7	6	11	8	6	1	0	*	4	3
GCE A level or equivalent	9	9	8	9	9	10	5	2	*	3	7
Trade apprenticeship	2	2	1	1	1	1	0	0	*	2	0
GCE O level/equivalent	36	36	25	31	21	27	14	15	*	41	27
CSE (not grade 1)	14	14	12	19	12	11	9	7	*	2	13
Other	3	3	6	3	10	6	5	10	*	12	8
None	18	18	29	16	21	22	58	53	*	20	24
(Never received any education)	0	0	3	0	1	0	14	5	*	3	1
Not stated/not known	1	1	1	2	1	2	2	2	*	0	1

Source: 1988, 1989, 1990 Labour Force Surveys (GB)

* Sample size too small

Column Percentages

Table 3.6 Highest qualification by ethnic group, 25-44 age group, 1988-90

	All origins	White	Total ethnic minority	Afro-Caribbean	African Asian	Indian	Pakistani	Bangla-deshi	Chinese	African	Other/Mixed
All Persons 25-44											
GCE A level/equivalent or higher	43	43	34	41	34	31	14	12	35	51	47
Of which: Degree/equivalent	11	11	12	5	14	14	5	6	15	16	19
Higher education below degree level	7	7	7	10	5	5	2	1	11	14	8
GCE A level/equivalent	25	26	16	26	15	12	7	5	9	21	20
Of which: BTEC(general)/ONC/OND	2	2	2	3	2	1	1	0	1	4	2
City & Guilds	11	11	5	12	4	3	2	1	1	6	6
GCE A level or equivalent	6	6	6	6	6	6	3	3	5	9	8
Trade apprenticeship	6	6	3	5	3	2	1	1	2	2	3
GCE O level/equivalent	17	18	13	18	19	11	5	5	7	18	12
CSE (not grade 1)	5	5	4	10	3	4	2	1	2	1	3
Other	7	6	12	6	15	12	12	10	10	13	18
None	27	27	35	23	27	39	65	71	44	15	20
(Never received any education)	0	0	4	0	1	3	16	15	6	2	1
Not stated/not known	1	1	2	2	2	3	2	1	2	1	1

Contd

Table 3.6 Highest qualification by ethnic group, 25-44 age group, 1988-90 (contd)

Column Percentages

	All origins	White	Total ethnic minority	Afro-Caribbean	African Asian	Indian	Pakistani	Bangla-deshi	Chinese	African	Other/Mixed
Men 25-44											
GCE A level/equivalent or higher	55	56	42	46	46	39	21	16	36	63	56
Of which: Degree/equivalent	13	13	15	7	18	16	6	7	19	24	23
Higher education below degree level	6	6	5	3	6	5	4	0	5	10	7
GCE A level/equivalent	36	37	22	36	22	17	12	9	1	29	26
Of which: BTEC(general)/ONC/OND	3	3	3	4	3	2	1	1	1	5	3
City & Guilds	18	18	8	19	6	5	5	2	2	7	10
GCE A level or equivalent	6	6	7	5	8	5	5	4	7	13	8
Trade apprenticeship	9	9	5	8	5	5	2	2	3	3	4
GCE O level/equivalent	11	11	9	14	14	8	4	3	6	13	7
CSE (not grade 1)	4	4	3	8	1	3	3	2	3	0	2
Other	6	6	12	6	15	11	10	14	10	11	18
None	23	22	31	24	22	34	58	64	43	11	16
(Never received any education)	0	0	2	0	1	2	6	3	5	0	1
Not stated/not known	1	1	3	2	2	5	3	1	2	2	2

Contd

53

Table 3.6   Highest qualification by ethnic group, 25-44 age group, 1988-90 (contd)

Column Percentages

	All origins	White	Total ethnic minority	Afro-Caribbean	African Asian	Indian	Pakistani	Bangla-deshi	Chinese	African	Other/Mixed
Women 25-44											
GCE A level/equivalent or higher	31	31	27	37	21	23	7	9	35	40	38
Of which: Degree/equivalent	8	8	9	4	10	11	4	5	12	8	14
Higher education below degree level	8	8	8	15	4	5	0	2	16	17	10
GCE A level/equivalent	14	14	10	18	7	7	2	2	6	15	14
Of which: BTEC(general)/ONC/OND	2	2	1	2	2	1	0	0	0	2	2
City & Guilds	4	4	2	5	1	0	0	0	0	5	2
GCE A level or equivalent	7	7	5	7	4	6	2	2	4	6	8
Trade apprenticeship	2	2	1	3	0	0	0	0	1	2	2
GCE O level/equivalent	23	24	15	22	23	13	5	7	8	22	16
CSE (not grade 1)	6	6	5	13	5	4	2	0	1	2	3
Other	7	7	13	5	15	14	13	7	10	15	18
None	32	32	39	22	33	44	71	77	45	20	24
(Never received any education)	0	0	7	0	1	5	26	24	6	3	1
Not stated/not known	1	1	1	1	2	1	2	0	2	1	0

Source: 1988, 1989, 1990 Labour Force Surveys (GB)

Table 3.7 Highest qualification by ethnic group, 45-59/64 age group, 1988-90

Column Percentages

	All origins	White	Total ethnic minority	Afro-Caribbean	African Asian	Indian	Pakistani	Bangla-deshi	Chinese	African	Other/Mixed
All Persons 45-59/64											
A level/equivalent or higher	33	33	27	30	25	27	13	11	20	55	35
Of which: Degree/equivalent	7	7	9	2	8	14	5	9	5	15	15
Higher education below degree level	6	6	6	10	3	4	1	1	5	16	6
GCE A level/equivalent	20	20	13	18	15	9	6	2	10	24	14
Of which: BTEC(general)/ONC/OND	1	1	1	0	0	1	0	0	2	4	1
City & Guilds	5	6	3	5	1	2	1	0	0	8	3
GCE A level or equivalent	3	3	4	2	9	5	4	1	4	8	4
Trade apprenticeship	10	11	6	12	5	2	2	1	4	4	6
GCE O level/equivalent	8	8	5	3	9	4	6	3	6	12	8
CSE (not grade 1)	0	0	0	0	0	1	1	0	0	0	0
Other	11	11	13	7	15	15	16	8	13	9	18
None	47	46	52	57	47	50	61	77	58	21	37
(Never recived any education)	1	0	11	2	3	14	31	28	13	4	3
Not stated/not known	1	1	3	3	2	3	3	1	3	3	2

Contd

Table 3.7 Highest qualification by ethnic group, 45-59/64 age group, 1988-90 (contd)

Column Percentages

	All origins	White	Total ethnic minority	Afro-Caribbean	African Asian	Indian	Pakistani	Bangla-deshi	Chinese	African	Other/Mixed
Men 45-64											
GCE A level/equivalent or higher	43	44	32	33	34	34	17	13	25	64	43
Of which: Degree/equivalent	9	9	11	3	10	17	7	10	6	22	20
Higher education below degree level	4	4	3	2	3	3	1	1	2	12	3
GCE A level/equivalent	30	30	19	28	21	14	9	2	16	31	21
Of which: BTEC(general)/ONC/OND	2	2	1	0	0	1	0	0	3	5	2
City & Guilds	8	9	4	8	1	3	1	0	0	9	5
GCE A level or equivalent	3	3	5	2	11	6	4	0	6	10	7
Trade apprenticeship	16	17	8	18	9	4	3	2	7	7	7
GCE O level/equivalent	6	6	5	2	11	3	6	5	7	12	8
CSE (not grade 1)	0	0	0	0	0	1	0	0	0	1	0
Other	10	10	14	7	17	17	20	11	13	5	14
None	39	39	45	54	34	39	52	70	52	15	32
(Never received any education)	0	0	7	3	2	8	18	20	7	1	3
Not stated/not known	1	1	4	4	3	5	4	1	3	3	3

Contd

Table 3.7 Highest qualification by ethnic group, 45-59/64 age group, 1988-90 (contd)

Column Percentages

	All origins	White	Total ethnic minority	Afro-Caribbean	African Asian	Indian	Pakistani	Bangla-deshi	Chinese	African	Other/Mixed
Women 45-59											
GCE A level/equivalent or higher	20	19	20	26	14	18	5	*	13	42	26
Of which: Degree/equivalent	4	3	6	2	4	10	2	*	2	6	10
Higher education below degree level	8	8	10	19	3	5	1	*	9	23	10
GCE A level/equivalent	8	8	5	5	6	3	2	*	2	13	6
Of which: BTEC (general)/ONC/OND	0	0	0	0	0	0	0	*	0	2	0
Gity & Guilds	2	2	1	1	0	0	0	*	0	7	0
GCE A level or equivalent	3	3	2	1	6	2	2	*	2	4	2
Trade apprenticeship	3	3	1	3	0	0	0	*	0	0	4
GCE O level/equivalent	11	12	5	4	7	6	5	*	4	12	8
CSE (not grade 1)	0	0	0	0	0	0	2	*	0	0	1
Other	12	12	11	7	12	11	7	*	12	14	24
None	56	55	62	61	65	64	80	*	69	31	41
(Never received any education)	1	0	17	1	5	23	57	*	22	9	4
Not stated/not known	1	1	1	1	2	1	1	*	2	1	0

Source: 1988, 1989, 1990 Labour Force Surveys (GB)

* Sample size too small

Table 3.8   Where gained highest qualification, 1988-90 (all ethnic minorities with qualifications)

Column Percentages

| | Highest qualification | | | | | | | |
	All quali-fications	A-level or higher	Degree/equivalent	Higher Ed. below degree	A-level/equivalent	O-level/equivalent	CSE/equivalent	Other
UK qualified	64	64	55	46	73	80	95	27
UK-born	32	27	14	16	37	50	59	8
Immigrant	32	37	41	30	36	30	36	19
Qualified abroad	36	36	45	54	27	20	5	73

Source: 1988, 1989, 1990 Labour Force Surveys (GB)

Table 3.9   Where gained highest qualification by ethnic group, 1988-90 (all ethnic minorities with qualifications)

Column Percentages

	Total ethnic minority	Afro-Caribbean	African Asian	Indian	Pakistani	Bangla-deshi	Chinese	African	Other/Mixed
UK qualified	64	77	61	60	65	60	59	53	60
Qualified abroad	36	23	39	40	35	40	41	47	40

Source: 1988, 1989, 1990 Labour Force Surveys (GB)

Table 3.10 Percentage who received some job-related training during the last four weeks by age and ethnic group, 1988-90 (employees, excluding government schemes)

Percentages

	Age 16-59/64			Age 16-24			Age 25-44			Age 45-59/64		
	All	M	F	All	M	F	All	M	F	All	M	F
All origins	14	14	14	21	23	19	15	15	15	8	7	9
White	14	14	14	21	23	19	15	15	15	8	8	9
Total ethnic minority	14	14	15	23	24	21	14	14	15	7	6	8
Afro-Caribbean	15	14	17	22	22	22	18	15	21	7	7	8
African Asian	12	12	13	24	27	22	11	10	12	4	5	*
Indian	11	11	12	21	23	18	11	11	10	5	3	9
Pakistani	10	10	11	19	22	*	8	8	*	4	4	*
Bangladeshi	8	4	*	7	*	*	*	*	*	*	*	*
Chinese	14	16	11	22	*	*	14	15	13	3	*	*
African	20	22	17	31	*	*	19	20	17	14	14	*
Other/Mixed	20	22	17	27	29	26	19	23	15	11	9	13

Source: 1988, 1989, 1990 Labour Force Surveys (GB)

* Sample size too small

59

Table 3.11 Percentage who received job-related training during the last four weeks by ethnic group and job level, 1988-90 (employees, excluding government schemes)

Percentages

	Professional/ Manager/Employer			Other non-manual			Skilled manual and Foreman			Semi-skilled manual			Unskilled manual		
	All	M	F	All	M	F	All	M	F	All	M	F	All	M	F
All origins	21	19	26	18	21	17	10	10	7	8	8	7	3	4	2
White	21	19	26	18	21	17	10	10	7	8	8	7	3	5	2
Total ethnic minority	21	19	25	21	25	19	9	9	7	6	5	7	3	4	3
Afro-Caribbean	29	29	30	22	24	21	10	11	*	8	4	10	3	*	3
African Asian	14	12	*	18	20	18	7	9	*	2	1	2	*	*	*
Indian	20	18	25	19	22	18	4	5	*	4	5	3	1	*	*
Pakistani	16	*	*	26	30	*	5	6	*	3	2	*	*	*	*
Bangladeshi	*	*	*	*	*	*	*	*	*	3	0	*	*	*	*
Chinese	11	*	*	19	*	16	*	*	*	12	15	*	*	*	*
African	23	*	*	25	31	21	17	*	*	10	7	12	*	*	*
Other/Mixed	24	23	*	21	27	17	20	16	*	12	12	12	*	*	*

Source: 1988, 1989, 1990 Labour Force Surveys (GB)

* Sample size too small

4 Employment

A number of factors led to the migration of people to Britain from its former colonies after the Second World War. Perhaps the most important was the contrast in terms of economic well-being between Britain and many of the countries it had colonised. People were attracted by the prospect of a higher standard of living, and more developed education and health systems. Because of specific labour shortages, affecting jobs then considered undesirable in some of the main conurbations, the early immigrants had very good prospects of finding work. Two further developments boosted immigration. First, the partition of India, which created a population of political and religious refugees who had a high incentive to emigrate. Second, from the late 1960s onwards the political persecution of South Asians living and working in East Africa created a new class of migrants. Among all of the incoming groups, it was young men who migrated first, although the pattern was especially marked in the case of South Asian people. This initial imbalance of the sexes was gradually redressed as wives and children of the young men who had pioneered the migration joined their husbands in Britain. There is a great deal of evidence showing that the life chances of these migrants were powerfully constrained by widespread racial discrimination. They tended to be in the more poorly-paid jobs which the indigenous population did not want, and had to live in cheap, low-quality housing.

The central part of this report is concerned with the position of ethnic minorities in the labour market. In particular, we are interested in the degree to which the early constraints mentioned above still exert an influence over the economic and social position of the ethnic minority populations today. A particular focus will be on the position of young people in the labour market, and how far their opportunities are constrained by their parents' situation in a social structure which was determined by conditions existing a generation ago.

Participation in the labour force
Men
Labour force participation rates are generally much higher for men than for women (see Table 4.1). A comparison of participation rates for men of working age show broadly similar rates for men of white and ethnic minority origins (taken together), 89 and 81 per cent respectively. Afro-Caribbean, African Asian and Indian men have rates nearer to those of whites, whereas men from the Pakistani, Bangladeshi, Chinese, African and Mixed/Other groups had lower rates (ranging between 70 and 79 per cent). As described in Chapter 2, the age structure of the ethnic minority population is a younger one than that of the indigenous population, and this partly explains the lower economic activity rates of the ethnic minority populations. Among men in the 16-24 age group, the rates are highest for white, Afro-Caribbean and Bangladeshi people (86, 78 and 77 per cent respectively), and lowest for Chinese and Pakistani men (49 and 55 per cent). In the middle age range of 25-44, rates of economic activity are high for men from all ethnic groups. Of white men 25-44, 97 per cent are either working or are seeking work, compared to 90 per cent of ethnic minority men. The highest labour force participation rate in this age group is amongst African Asian men, of whom 98 per cent are economically active. In the pre-retirement age group (45-64 for men), African Asian men have the highest activity rate of 90 per cent, compared to 81 per cent of whites. The activity rate for ethnic minorities as a whole, 83 per cent, is in fact higher in this age group than for white men.

Women
Table 4.1 shows large variations in the labour force participation rates between women of different ethnic origins. Taking all women of working age, Afro-Caribbeans have the highest proportion who are working or seeking work: 76 per cent compared to 71 per cent of white women. African Asian women have a similar participation rate to whites (69 per cent), and African, Indian and Chinese women have somewhat lower rates (61, 57 and 55 per cent respectively). The main feature of the overall participation rates for women is the very low rates for Pakistani and Bangladeshi women, both 23 per cent, reflecting the low proportion of women from thse groups who work outside the home.

As shown in Chapter 2, the ethnic minority populations have, in general, a younger age distribution than the indigenous population. This helps explain a part of the lower average rates of economic activity among women in some ethnic groups, but analysis within age groups shows that substantial differences remain. Within the 16-24 age group, white and Afro-Caribbean women have the highest participation rates, while Pakistani and Bangladeshi women have by far the lowest rates. This disparity is widest in the middle age range 25-44, in which about three quarters of white, African Asian and Afro-Caribbean women are seeking work or working. Indian, African and Chinese women have slightly lower participation rates of around 60 per cent, but are substantially more likely to be participating in the labour market than are Pakistani and Bangladeshi women in this age group. Of these two groups, 19 and 22 per cent respectively are economically active. In general, economic activity rates fall for women of most ethnic origins in the pre-retirement age group of 45-59. The exceptions to this are the rates for women of Afro-Caribbean and African origin, which rise to 83 per cent and 78 per cent respectively (compared to 67 per cent for whites). Pakistani women in this age group again have a very low rate of labour force participation, of only 13 per cent.

Table 4.2 shows that women's economic activity rate varies according to whether or not they have dependent children in quite a different way for different ethnic groups. This suggests that a large part of variation in economic activity rates for women of different ethnic origins is due to differences in culture concerning the role of women in home-making and child-rearing. Afro-Caribbean women have relatively high rates of economic activity whether or not they are married or cohabiting or have dependent children. Pakistani and Bangladeshi women have much lower rates of economic activity than women of other groups, and this is true of both married and unmarried women. The differences become sharper when we compare women with dependent children, but the basic pattern remains. This reflects the traditionally important economic role played by Afro-Caribbean women; by contrast, within the Pakistani and Bangladeshi traditions, women are less likely to work outside the home. This is confirmed by Table 4.3, which shows a much higher proportion of Pakistani and Bangladeshi women than of women from other ethnic groups looking after the home and family. Another reason for relatively lower participation rates amongst some ethnic minority groups is the greater proportion of ethnic minorities in full-time education (see Chapter 3).

Young people in the labour market
Table 4.3 shows economic activity for men and women in the 16-24 age band. As mentioned above, for both men and women, economic activity rates in this age group are considerably lower for South Asians (especially Pakistanis and Bangladeshis) than for white people, and slightly lower for Afro-Caribbeans, too. A major reason for these relatively low rates of economic activity among young people belonging to ethnic minorities is

their greater propensity to remain in full-time education than members of the indigenous population. Another factor is that many young women of Pakistani and Bangladeshi origin are not available for work due to domestic and family responsibilities.

Young men of white and Afro-Caribbean origin are probably more likely than those belonging to other ethnic groups to be employed on government schemes, mostly on the Youth Training Scheme (YTS).[1] About 6 per cent of white and Afro-Caribbean men aged 16-24 are employed on government schemes, compared to 5 per cent of Pakistani, and 4 per cent of Indian and African Asian men. Of African men in the 16-24 age range, 2 per cent are on government schemes, whereas none of the Bangladeshi or Chinese men of this age group in the LFS sample reported that they were employed on such schemes. For young women, those of white and Pakistani origin were slightly more likely to be employed on government schemes than women of other origins, but the proportions involved are in all cases very small.

The Youth Cohort Study (YCS) provides more detailed information about young ethnic minority people in the labour market.[2] The take-up of YTS places at 16 was found to be similar for the white and Afro-Caribbean groups, but much lower for South Asians. Whilst over 30 per cent of the white and Afro-Caribbean cohorts took up YTS places, only about one in ten of the South Asian cohort did so. The YCS shows only small numbers of ethnic minority people entering employment at this stage relative to young white people, regardless of the level of attainment that has been reached. Drew, Gray, and Sime constructed models of the probability of taking up a place on YTS at 16. They found that local labour markets had a strong effect, in that young people were more likely to take up a YTS place in areas of high unemployment. When the effect of local labour markets was removed, ethnic origin was found to be a significant factor in YTS take-up, along with attainment and social class. The same authors examined variations in the destinations of leavers three months after the end of YTS. A lower proportion of Afro-Caribbean and South Asian young people were found to be in employment after YTS than of whites.

Full or part-time working
In general, women are much more likely than men to be in part-time jobs,[3] as Table 4.4 shows. White women are generally more likely than women from other racial groups to be working part-time, whereas the pattern is reversed for male employees (although amongst male employees from all ethnic origins, rates of part-time working are generally very low).

Of the white female population of working age, 26 per cent are in part-time work, which is a higher proportion than for any other ethnic group. Within the minority population, African women are the most likely to be in part-time jobs, with 17 per cent in this category. Afro-Caribbean and African Asian women have a similar proportion in part-time work (16 and 15 per cent respectively). Chinese and Indian women also have a similar likelihood of being in part-time employment, with 14 and 13 per cent respectively. Pakistani and Bangladeshi women are the least likely to be in part-time jobs, with about 4 and 5 per cent respectively in this category, but this reflects their low participation rate more generally.

Self-employment

Table 4.4 shows that a larger proportion of the populations of South Asian and Chinese origin describe themselves as self-employed than of people from other ethnic groups. Taking all people of working age, the most likely groups to be self-employed are the Chinese, of whom 19 per cent reported that they were in this category, compared to 9 per cent of the white population of working age. People of Indian and African Asian ethnic origin have higher proportions of self-employed than the whites, 13 and 14 per cent respectively. Pakistanis have a similar likelihood to whites of being self-employed, and Bangladeshis a slightly lower one (7 per cent). However, Afro-Caribbean and African people have the lowest probability of being self-employed, with 6 and 4 per cent of their respective populations in this category. The pattern is similar for both male and female populations, although a higher proportion of the male population of working age from all ethnic groups reported that they were self-employed.

Table 4.5 shows the distribution of self-employed between different industry sectors. White and Afro-Caribbean self-employed are likely to be in the construction industry, which accounts for 24 per cent of the white, and 34 per cent of the Afro-Caribbean self-employed, compared to much smaller proportions of other racial groups. The highest concentration of self-employed from all racial groups is found in division 6 which covers distribution, hotels, repairs and catering. This division takes up 23 per cent of white, and 56 per cent of ethnic minority self-employed. Within the South Asian and Chinese groups there is an even higher concentration of self-employed in this division. Retail distribution accounts for a large part of self-employment in the African Asian, Indian and Pakistani working populations (58, 51 and 46 per cent respectively). Three quarters of the Chinese self-employed are to be found in the hotel and catering trade. It is striking that a fifth of the Pakistani self-employed have businesses in the transport and communications sector, compared to one in twenty of the

65

white self-employed; and a tenth or more of the white, African Asian, and Indian self-employed are within the banking and finance industry.

Although the rate of self-employment is higher among ethnic minorities than among white people, and although self-employed people from ethnic minorities are concentrated in a few industries, nevertheless the great majority of people belonging to ethnic minorities are employees, and these employees are distributed over a wider range of industries. Hence the pattern of self-employment is not the dominant factor in shaping the overall pattern. For example, whilst 72 per cent of the African Asian self-employed are found in the distribution, hotels, catering and repairs trade, this sector accounts for a much smaller proportion of all African Asians in work (33 per cent).

Of the self-employed, Afro-Caribbeans are the least likely to have employees (only 17 per cent have staff), while the Chinese and Bangladeshis are most likely to be employing staff (62 and 67 per cent respectively, see Table 4.6). Only a very small proportion of the self-employed from any ethnic group have 25 or more employees, and there is very little difference between the respective proportions of the various ethnic groups that come into this category.

Industry sector

Previous research on ethnic minorities and the labour market has found a marked concentration of ethnic minority people in employment in certain industries. It is important to see how structural changes in the UK economy over the 1980s have affected this distribution. For example, there has been a dramatic fall in the proportion of the British workforce which is employed in manufacturing and heavy industry, and an expansion of the private services sector.

Taking all dependent employees, the biggest proportion of both white and ethnic minority workers is accounted for by distribution, hotels, catering and repairs. One fifth of all white, and over a fifth of ethnic minority employees work in this industry (see Table 4.7). There is a relatively high concentration of South Asian employees in retail distribution, which accounts for 18 per cent of African Asian employees, for 11 per cent of both Pakistani and Indian employees, and for 11 per cent of white employees, too. Chinese and Bangladeshi people are particularly concentrated in hotels and catering, which accounts for 38 and 41 per cent of employees from these groups, but for only 4 per cent of white employees.

Afro-Caribbeans are more likely than employees from other ethnic groups to be found in the transport and communication sector, which accounts for over a tenth of Afro-Caribbean employees compared to 6 per cent of whites. There are particularly high concentrations of Afro-Caribbean and African employees working in the 'other services' sector (36 and 44 per cent of each group respectively compared to 29 per cent of whites). In particular, Afro-Caribbeans and Africans are well-represented in hospitals and medical care institutions compared with other groups. Whereas 5 per cent of white employees work in hospitals and similar institutions, 14 per cent of African and 13 per cent of Afro-Caribbean employees work in such places (and also 13 per cent of Chinese employees).

When these comparisons are made for men and women separately, a broadly similar picture emerges, although the degree of concentration in certain sectors is greater in some cases. The main themes are again quite clearly seen in Tables 4.8 and 4.9; namely, the importance of retail distribution in the African Asian and Indian populations, the high concentration of Bangladeshi (male) and Chinese (male and female) employees in the restaurant sector, the relative importance of construction as a source of employment for Afro-Caribbean men and of health services for Afro-Caribbean and African women.

Taking all male employees (Table 4.8), there is a notable concentration of men of African Asian ethnic origin in the retail distribution sector. There is also a relatively high concentration of ethnic minority men in the 'other manufacturing' sector, particularly of Pakistani men, with 32 per cent of all Pakistani male employees found here (13 per cent in textiles), compared to 11 per cent of white men. Of all Bangladeshi male employees, 15 per cent work in clothing and footwear. White and Afro-Caribbean men are relatively more likely to work in the construction industry. There are very high proportions of the Bangladeshi and Chinese working male population in the hotels and catering sector; 50 and 43 per cent respectively compared to just 2 per cent of white male employees. The tendency for Afro-Caribbean men to have jobs in transport and communication is reflected in the high proportion (17 per cent) of Afro-Caribbean male employees in this sector, a proportion which is almost double that for whites. African Asian men have a relatively high likelihood of being found in the banking and finance industry: this sector accounts for 14 per cent of male employees, compared to about 10 per cent of whites.

For women employees (Table 4.9), there is also a high concentration in the distribution, hotels, catering and repairs sector, with a quarter of white and over a fifth of ethnic minority women employees working there. The proportions of Pakistani and Chinese women employees working in shops, hotels and restaurants are particularly high (32 and 41 per cent respectively), whereas the corresponding proportion of Afro-Caribbean women is lower than for all other groups, including white women. Pakistani and African Asian women are particularly likely to work in retail distribution, which accounts for 23 and 19 per cent of women employees from these groups. There is not the same concentration of ethnic minority women workers in the hotel and catering trade as is the case for men, with the notable exception of Chinese women, among whom 33 per cent of employees work in this sector (compared to 7 per cent of female white employees). The female working population as a whole is most concentrated into division 9 ('other services') which accounts for 41 per cent of white, and 40 per cent of ethnic minority women employees. There are particularly high concentrations of Afro-Caribbean and African women working in this sector, which accounts for more than half of all women employees from each group. A substantial part of this concentration is explained by the high proportion of some groups working in hospitals or other medical institutions. Compared to 9 per cent of white women employees, 22 per cent of Afro-Caribbean and African, and 19 per cent of Chinese women employees work in health care institutions.

More localised analyses would reveal a greater concentration of employees in particular industry sectors. For example, the SCPR survey of Scottish ethnic minorities found that 45 per cent of male ethnic minority householders who were employees worked in the distribution, hotels, catering and repairs sector, compared with 11 per cent of their white counterparts. Similarly, female ethnic minority employees were also more likely than whites to work in this sector, with 47 and 23 per cent respectively of these groups found there.

Job levels
A recurring theme of all the previous studies of ethnic minorities in the British labour market is their relative concentration in the lower level and more poorly-paid jobs compared to the white labour force. This was one of the central findings of the *Black and White Britain* survey, and even when the effect of qualifications was controlled, Afro-Caribbean and South Asian people tended to be in substantially lower job levels than whites. We have already referred to the changes in employment patterns in the UK economy, with a general shift away from heavy industry and manufacturing and towards the service sector. There have been some moves in recent years aimed at encouraging equal opportunities in recruitment and the promotion of fairer personnel practices. As we saw in the section on self-employment, the high proportion of self-employed amongst economically active African Asian and Indian men in particular may reflect a growing development of business networks amongst these groups. Some sources have suggested that

such networks may well generate employment within certain minority populations.[4] The question to which we now turn is the extent to which these and other developments have affected the overall distribution of workers from the various ethnic groups between different job levels.

Definitions

In order to be able to make firm comparisons, the present analysis adopts the same schema for job levels that was used in PSI survey of 1982. This is a grouping into five categories of the 17 socio-economic groups defined by OPCS for use in the census and in government surveys (see Appendix 4).

Men

Table 4.10 shows that a complex pattern is developing, with some minority groups having similar (or higher) job levels than white male employees, whereas other groups have substantially lower ones. In general, African Asian, Indian and Chinese male employees have similar or better job levels than white male employees. In fact, there are more of the Chinese in the top category (professional, managerial, employer) than there are of whites: 30 per cent compared with 27 per cent. African Asians have the same proportion as whites in the top category, and Indians have a similar proportion (25 per cent). This finding is so striking that it is worth considering separately the main components of the top category. The table shows that more of the Chinese, African Asian and Indian male employees are in professional jobs than is the case for whites: in fact, Chinese male employees are twice as likely as whites to be in professional jobs. By contrast, the bulk of the white employment in this top category consists of men employed as managers in large establishments, who account for 13 per cent of all white male employees. It seems, therefore, that men from certain minority groups have penetrated to a remarkable extent into certain professions, but to a much lesser extent into the senior management of large organisations.

Whilst there is strong evidence that in the case of men certain minority groups have achieved parity with white men in terms of the proportion within the top of the five broad job levels, there is equally strong evidence that certain other minority groups remain at substantially lower job levels than whites. The proportion of Afro-Caribbean, Pakistani and Bangladeshi male employees in the top category is less than half of that of whites (12 per cent for each of the three groups, compared with 27 per cent for whites). Afro-Caribbeans and Pakistanis are the most likely to be found in skilled manual work, with 39 and 34 per cent respectively of their male employees in such jobs. A very high proportion of Bangladeshi men are employed in semi-skilled or unskilled manual jobs (70 per cent of Bangladeshi men, compared with 19 per cent of whites). The 1986 Home Affairs Committee report on the Bangladeshi population in Britain remarked on the particularly low job levels held by Bangladeshi men compared to men from other ethnic groups. Another important feature is the apparent polarisation of some of the minority groups, which have high proportions in both the upper and lower categories, compared to whites. Whilst a relatively high proportion of Indian and Chinese male employees are found in the top category, there are also high proportions of these employees in semi-skilled and unskilled manual jobs (28 and 40 per cent respectively). This may suggest that men from these two groups enter a relatively narrow range of occupations, either at the top or bottom end of the job market. South Asians, with the exception of African Asians, are generally more likely to be in lower manual jobs than are whites.

Whilst the SCPR survey on ethnic minorities in Scotland found that there were no large differences in the job levels of female employees of different ethnic groups, it found a relatively high proportion of male ethnic minority employees in the top job category. Results were given for the job levels of Indian, Pakistani and Chinese people, as well as whites. A slightly different pattern emerges than that from the LFS, with Chinese male householders who are employees having the same proportion (25 per cent) as whites in the professional/manager/employer category. Pakistani men have a higher proportion than white in the top category (28 per cent). The group with the highest proportion of male employees in the top category is the Indians, with 41 per cent described as professional/manager/employer. So compared to the LFS, SCPR's Scottish survey found relatively fewer Chinese male employees in the top category and substantially more Pakistanis. Some of the differences may be accounted for by the fact that the LFS results are based on individuals, whereas the SCPR survey covers householders. Nevertheless, these results still provide additional evidence that some ethnic minority groups are increasingly represented in the higher job levels.

Women

All previous research on the position of ethnic minorities in the labour market has found that there is much less disparity between women employees of different ethnic groups than is the case for men. The present study makes a similar finding, as is illustrated by Table 4.11. This shows smaller proportions of women employees than of men in the top category, but Indian and white women have similar proportions in the top group (10 and 11 per cent), and Chinese women employees have a higher proportion

(16 per cent). The largest proportion of women employees of all ethnic origins are found in the other non-manual section, with about half (or in some cases more) female employees from all ethnic groups. So the distribution of job levels between female employees of different ethnic groups is more compressed than that of males. The explanation which is generally given for this pattern is that because of discrimination, and because of structural factors associated with the family, women of all ethnic groups are confined to a much narrower range of opportunities than are men. This means that the processes of racial disadvantage have much less room in which to operate.

Job levels and qualifications

One explanation for the differences in job levels between people of different ethnic origins could be that (as shown in Chapter 3) they have different levels of formal qualification. Tables 4.12 and 4.13 analyse the job levels of different ethnic groups within certain qualification bands.

Men

Chinese, Indian and African Asian male employees whose highest qualification is A level or equivalent or above are all more likely to be in the top (Professional, Manager or Employer) category than are whites. Of these groups, 48, 45, and 42 per cent respectively are in the top category compared to 37 per cent of whites. There is a somewhat lower proportion of Pakistani male employees with such qualifications in the top category (30 per cent), and a substantially lower proportion of Afro-Caribbeans than of any other group (23 per cent). Looking within this category, highly qualified male employees of all ethnic groups except the Afro-Caribbeans are more likely than whites to be in professional jobs. Afro-Caribbean men with highest qualifications at this level are in lower job levels than men of other ethnic groups.

Of male employees qualified up to and including O level or CSE standard or holding some other qualification, white men are clearly in higher job levels than ethnic minority men. Over a fifth are in the top category, which is higher than for South Asian men, and substantially higher than for Afro-Caribbean men (of whom 7 per cent are in such jobs). In other job levels at this qualification level, the variation between ethnic groups is not so great.

Of those male employees with no formal qualifications, Afro-Caribbeans and Bangladeshis are more often found at lower job levels than employees of other ethnic groups. White and African Asian non-qualified employees are at similar job levels, in both cases higher than for non-qualified employees from other ethnic groups. Of non-qualified white and African Asian employees, 11 and 8 per cent respectively are in the top category, compared to 3 per cent of Afro-Caribbean and of Bangladeshi non-qualified employees.

Women

Analysis of job levels within qualification bands for women employees (Table 4.13) again shows less variation between ethnic groups than for men. In the higher qualification band (A-level or equivalent and above), Chinese and Indian women have the highest proportion in the top group: 28 and 25 per cent of female employees respectively, compared to 22 per cent of whites. There is not much variation by ethnic group at other job levels.

Of women employees with O level, CSEs or other qualifications, or no qualifications, there is not much variation in job level between women of different ethnic groups, although slightly more of the whites are in higher jobs.

Job levels and foreign qualifications

In Chapter 3, we found that 64 per cent of ethnic minority people with qualifications in the Britain gained them after coming to the country. It is important to establish whether UK-qualified ethnic minority people are at different job levels from those who qualified abroad. Because of sample sizes, the best that can be done is to examine the circumstances of all male employees with qualifications. In Table 4.14, the job levels of ethnic minority male employees with UK and foreign qualifications are compared. For some groups, those who qualified in the UK are at slightly higher job levels overall. For example, a greater proportion of Afro-Caribbean men who qualified in the UK are in the professional/manager/employer category (17 per cent), than are those who qualified abroad (13 per cent), but the difference is not large. A similar pattern is apparent for African Asians, but for Indians, Africans and Pakistanis the position is different. Although again the differences are not large, bigger proportions of the men in these groups who qualified abroad are in the top category than from the UK-qualified. The differences at other job levels are not great, and no clear pattern emerges. There is no clear evidence from this analysis that employers tend to put a higher value on UK rather than foreign qualifications.

Labour market mobility

In order to assess mobility in and out of employment we compared the positions of white and ethnic minority men and women in the 25-44 age range at the time of the interview and one year before. For men, there was not a great deal of difference between whites and ethnic minorities. Of those presently not in work (unemployed or inactive), 29 per cent of white men had been in work one year before, compared with 26 per cent for ethnic minority men. Of those who had not been in work a year earlier, 34 per cent of the white men were currently in work, compared to 27 per cent of ethnic minority men.

White women showed greater mobility in and out of employment than ethnic minority women. Of those not in work at the time of the interview, 15 per cent of whites had been in work a year earlier, compared to 10 per cent of ethnic minorities. Of those women in work at the time of the interview, 22 per cent of the whites and 14 per cent of the ethnic minorities had not been in work a year earlier.

Two other measures of mobility within the labour market have also been considered: mobility between employers, and between jobs. Table 4.15 shows mobility *between employers* of prime age employees belonging to the various ethnic groups. The proportion of employees working for a different firm compared with a year earlier did not vary greatly between ethnic groups, but the Bangladeshi, African and Chinese employees were the most likely to be working in a different firm (18 or 19 per cent, compared with 13 per cent of whites). Afro-Caribbeans were also more likely than whites to be in a different firm (16 per cent). Mobility between employers was about the same among African Asians as among whites, but slightly lower among Pakistanis. This pattern is the same for prime age women and men, although women are less likely on the whole to have moved firms.

Table 4.16 shows job mobility *between jobs* for prime age employees. This reveals that Afro-Caribbeans and whites are more likely than other groups to have changed jobs in the last year. Among employees in work both at the time of the interview and a year earlier, 16 per cent of Afro-Caribbeans and 15 per cent of whites were in different jobs from the previous year. The proportion in a different job from a year before was slightly lower in the case of African Asian and Indians (13 and 11 per cent), but considerably lower in the case of Pakistanis and Bangladeshis (10 and 7 per cent respectively). A similar pattern appears for both men and women, although more of the women are in a different job from the previous year.

Hours and shiftwork
Table 4.17 shows the mean number of hours worked in the reference week, by employees of different ethnic groups. There is not a great deal of variation between full-time employees of different ethnic groups, although for both men and women, the Chinese worked the highest number of hours on average. The variation is greater amongst part-time female employees;

white women working part-time put in fewer hours on average than women belonging to other ethnic groups (although the sample sizes are too small to make comments about Pakistani, Bangladeshi, Chinese or African part-time women workers as separate groups). The SCPR Scottish study found that ethnic minority employees tended to work longer weekly hours than whites. Like the LFS, the SCPR study found that Chinese employees worked longer weekly hours than employees of other ethnic groups.

Taken together, ethnic minority employees are more likely to be doing shiftwork than are white employees (Table 4.18). More of the Pakistanis are doing shifts than any other group, with 33 per cent employed on this kind of work, compared to 15 per cent of white employees. Employees from the other ethnic groups are slightly more likely than whites to be engaged on shiftwork, with the exception of African Asian employees, of whom 14 per cent are in this category.

The probability of ethnic minority employees being engaged in shiftwork rises sharply with age. Among those aged 16-24, 13 per cent do shifts compared with 11 per cent of whites. This rises to 21 per cent in the 25-44 age range (16 per cent for whites), and to 27 per cent in the 45-59/64 group (14 per cent of whites). In all ethnic groups except the Chinese, male are more likely than female employees to be engaged on shiftwork.

Among male dependent employees of working age, the proportion working shifts is lowest among those of Chinese origin (14 per cent, compared with 18 per cent of whites). The other ethnic groups have a higher likelihood of working shifts, and this increases in the older age groups. For example, whilst 12 per cent of Afro-Caribbean male employees in the 16-24 age group are engaged on shiftwork, this rises to 21 and 40 per cent in the middle and pre-retirement age groups. A similar pattern is observable for Indian and Pakistani male employees, with the proportion doing shift work substantially less in the 16-24 age group. In fact, the group that stands out overall is male employees of Pakistani origin, of whom 40 per cent are doing shiftwork. In all age groups, Pakistani male employees are always substantially more likely to be doing shiftwork than employees of other origins.

Among female employees of working age, the proportion working shifts is highest among those of Afro-Caribbean and Chinese origin (19 and 18 per cent respectively, compared with 11 per cent of whites). The proportion doing shiftwork is also slightly higher among women of African origin than among whites, but it is lower among those of South Asian origin. Among female employees in the 16-24 age group, the proportion doing shiftwork is highest among Afro-Caribbean women (13 per cent) than among any other ethnic group. In fact Afro-Caribbean women have the highest probability of doing shift work in all age groups except for the middle age band of 25-44, in which Chinese women have a slightly higher probability. For all women employees from racial minority groups, the likelihood of being in shiftwork increases with age. For white women employees, the proportion doing shiftwork falls from 12 per cent in the 16-24 age group to 9 per cent in the 45-59 group. The opposite effect occurs for Afro-Caribbean women (for whom the corresponding figures are 13 and 23 per cent) and Indian women (6 to 12 per cent). The sample sizes for women of other ethnic minority groups are too small to break down by age group in this case.

These results suggest that younger people belonging to ethnic minority groups are not following the older generations into the kinds of jobs which involve shiftwork.

Establishment size
Table 4.19 shows a very basic breakdown of workplace establishment size for employees of all ethnic groups. Because people cannot estimate the size of their workplace very accurately, LFS respondents are only asked whether the establishment has 25 or more employees, or fewer. For all employees of working age, most work in establishments of 25 or more employees. This is the case for employees of all ethnic origins with the notable exceptions of Bangladeshi and Chinese employees. Whereas 67 per cent of white and 71 per cent of all ethnic minority employees are found in workplaces of 25 or over, 47 per cent of Chinese and only 34 per cent of Bangladeshi employees are in such workplaces. This pattern remains the same for both sexes and across all age groups. In general, younger employees, and women, have a greater probability of working in smaller establishments.

Trade union membership
The LFS has included a question on trade union membership since 1989, so the findings presented here are based on an average of the data for 1989-90 rather then on the usual 3 year average.

A general theme of research on the UK labour market over the 1980s was the marked decline in trade union membership. This was seen as resulting from two main factors. First, the massive decline in employment in areas of relative union strength such as manufacturing and heavy industry. Second, the effect of legislation by successive governments hostile to trade union power and organisation. There is still a great deal of debate about the extent to which the union decline was an irreversible development of UK industrial relations, or whether it was in the main a temporary phenomenon related to economic recession. The interest of the present study surrounds the different union membership rates amongst employees of the various minority ethnic groups compared to whites. The PEP survey of 1974 and the PSI survey of 1982 found that union membership rates were higher amongst Afro-Caribbeans and South Asians than amongst whites, even after controlling for job level.

Table 4.20 shows trade union membership rates for employees (excluding government schemes) by sex and age groups. We found earlier that white, African Asian, Indian and Chinese employees are often in relatively high job levels, and that Afro-Caribbean and Pakistani (as well as Bangladeshi) employees are relatively well-represented in lower manual occupations. This would lead us to expect higher than average union membership rates amongst the latter groups.

Taking overall rates of union membership, Afro-Caribbean employees have the highest rate compared with employees of other ethnic groups. Of all Afro-Caribbean employees, 44 per cent are union members compared to 35 per cent of white employees. Indian employees also have a higher membership rate than whites, with 38 per cent of employees being union members. Pakistani employees have a slightly lower rate than whites (33 per cent), as do African Asian employees (28 per cent). Very low rates of union membership are apparent amongst Chinese and Bangladeshi employees (19 and 14 per cent respectively). Among employees of all ethnic origins, union membership rates are substantially higher in the older age bands.

Men

Men are generally more likely than women to be members of a trade union, with the exception of the African and Chinese groups, where the position is reversed. For all male employees, we see a move away from the earlier patterns of higher union membership amongst South Asians than amongst whites. Indian employees are still slightly more likely than whites to be members of trade unions (42 per cent compared with 40 per cent). However, Pakistani (36 per cent), African Asian (32 per cent), and Bangladeshi (12 per cent) employees all have lower rates than the whites. The highest rates are found amongst Afro-Caribbean employees, of whom 48 per cent are union members. A similar pattern occurs for employees in all age groups, with the rates being substantially higher in the older age groups.

The SCPR study in Scotland differed from the LFS in that (as we would expect) it showed a higher membership rate for white male employees (53 per cent) than the national figure. On the whole, the Scottish survey found that ethnic minority employees are less likely than whites to be members of trade unions. The rate for South Asian male employees (taken together) is given as 39 per cent, and that for Chinese male employees is just 7 per cent.

Women

For women employees, Afro-Caribbeans have the highest union membership rate by a considerable margin; 41 per cent compared to 29 per cent of white women. African and Indian women also have higher membership rates than do the whites (33 and 32 per cent respectively). African Asian, Chinese and Pakistani women have lower rates of membership, although the variation is less than amongst men. Small sample sizes prevent a detailed analysis by age group of the female union membership rates for some minority groups. However, Afro-Caribbean women have the highest rates in all age groups, peaking at 55 per cent in the 45-59 group (compared to 34 per cent of whites). Indian women also show higher rates of union membership than whites. Both these findings may be partly explained by the relatively high concentration of Afro-Caribbean and Indian women employees in highly-unionised health services (see earlier section).

Analysis by job level

One possible explanation for differing rates of union membership between different ethnic groups is the different job levels held by employees from the various ethnic groups. Table 4.21 shows union membership rates for the different ethnic populations within job levels. Within job levels, the variation between ethnic groups is less, but the relatively higher proportion of Afro-Caribbean employees who are union members, compared with other ethnic groups, still stands out.

The secondary sector

During the 1980s, a number of authors proposed that the labour market was becoming increasingly polarised between a primary sector, in which jobs are stable, full-time and offer prospects of progression and training, and a secondary sector, in which jobs are often temporary, seasonal, or part-time, tend to be low-paid, and offer little prospect of training or advancement. Thus, a dual labour market develops, with a core of better-paid, more highly trained, permanent employees, and a periphery of poorly-paid, temporary or casual workers. Previous research has suggested that the ethnic minority workforce is concentrated within this 'secondary' sector. In addition, it has been argued that ethnic minorities are over-represented in the declining industries in the manufacturing sector, and that this helps to explain the higher rates of unemployment amongst ethnic minorities than amongst the white population. We will be considering the different rates of unemployment between the various ethnic groups in detail in the next chapter, but the ideas expressed above are clearly relevant to employment as well as unemployment. We have constructed a rough measure of this secondary sector to see whether the LFS data shows a higher concentration of ethnic minority employees than of white employees there (see Table 4.22). We have taken the secondary sector to include the other manufacturing and distribution, repairs, hotels and catering sectors (because many of the periphery-type jobs are found here), the small firm sector, temporary, seasonal or casual jobs, and fixed-period jobs. The table shows that Afro-Caribbean and African employees are less likely than employees from other ethnic groups to be working in the secondary sector on this definition. Similar proportions of these two groups are found here: 44 and 43 per cent respectively, compared with 53 per cent of white employees. The proportion of African Asian and Indian employees in the secondary sector is the same as for white employees, whereas the proportion of Pakistani, Chinese, and Bangladeshi employees is higher (63, 66 and 80 per cent respectively). Thus, bearing in mind that we are able to adopt only a rough definition of the secondary sector, only one of the ethnic minority groups – Bangladeshis – is highly concentrated within it. Other minority groups are represented in the secondary sector either at about the same level as whites, or at a considerably lower level.

Earnings
Research into earnings differentials in Britain has tended to concentrate on inequalities between men and women rather than those between different ethnic groups. This is partly because of the lack of suitable data; the LFS has only included a question about earnings since 1991, and the New Earnings Survey contains no information about ethnic origin. Research in the USA has found that members of ethnic minority groups (particularly African American men) experience a substantial shortfall in earnings which is accounted for by discrimination.[5] *Black and White Britain* collected information on the earnings of ethnic minority groups in 1982. This showed that overall, Afro-Caribbean and South Asian men earned about 15 per cent less than white men. Even when comparisons were made within job levels and age groups, part of this gap still persisted. Additionally, the study found that Indians and African Asians earned more than Afro-Caribbeans, and Pakistanis and Bangladeshis less. However, it also found that there was little difference between the earnings of ethnic minority and white women. Other research has made use of the National Training Survey,[6] the GHS,[7] and special surveys of particular groups.[8] What is remarkable is the lack of

significant up-to-date research on the subject; the GHS-based studies (with one exception) use data from 1972, and that using the National Training Survey draws on data from 1975. Even the most recent econometric studies are based on data from the early 1980s.

The concentration of ethnic minority households in the main conurbations suggests the need for analysis at a more local level. Local labour markets have distinctive conditions which cannot be controlled for at the national level. It is also more likely that racial wage differentials amongst the participants in the same local labour market will be more significant than national differentials in producing a feeling of injustice and resentment. McCormick compared data collected in 1982-83 in the West Midlands and Greater London.[9] He found that in certain areas of Birmingham, both Afro-Caribbean and South Asian heads of household had significantly lower average weekly earnings (before overtime) than their white counterparts (other things being equal). The average earnings difference between whites and ethnic minorities was estimated at between 10 and 13 per cent. A significantly larger racial earnings differential was found in Greater London than in the West Midlands; over 30 per cent as compared with 7 per cent. More recently, the London Living Standards Survey found that in 1986, white men tended to earn about 15 per cent more than men from the ethnic minorities. A local survey carried out in Leicester during 1990[10] showed that male South Asian workers earned about 80 per cent of the earnings of white workers.

There have been very few studies concentrating on particular segments of the labour market. However, the follow-up study of 1980 graduates carried out by the Education and Employment Departments did distinguish between white and non-white.[11] It suggested that white graduates received lower earnings than non-white graduates, although the authors stressed the small sample size for the non-whites, which weakened the reliability of the findings, and prevented the analysis of possible differences between specific ethnic minority groups. The main reason for the unexpected finding was that non-white graduates were more likely to have studied subjects which tend to be more rewarding in terms of earnings. For example, non-whites had a relatively high representation in engineering and economics, and a relatively low one in the arts.

At present, there is only the limited evidence of a few local studies on which to assess the likely changes in earnings differentials between ethnic groups in recent years. These studies suggest that the differences are still substantial, but at present we have no data to compare with the analysis in *Black and White Britain.*

Earnings are a central part of the labour market experience of any individual, and earlier studies found that to a large extent racial disadvantage in the labour market was reflected in earnings. The lack of information about the earnings of ethnic minorities at the end of the 1980s constitutes an important gap in what we know about their relative labour market position. Such information is essential in order to put into context some of the developments so far described, such as the improved educational performance and job levels of some ethnic minority groups.

The pattern of change
The PEP and PSI surveys of 1974 and 1982 showed in broad terms that South Asian and Afro-Caribbean men tended to occupy considerably poorer positions in the labour market than white men. The new LFS analysis suggests that by around 1989, the specific minority groups had tended to diverge. Certain groups – the African Asians and Indians, in particular – had come to occupy a labour market position hardly inferior to that of whites. Other groups – especially the Bangladeshis, and to a lesser extent the Pakistanis – continued to occupy a very much poorer position.

The proportion participating in the labour force tends to be lower among ethnic minority men than among whites, even within age groups. In the case of the young, this is largely because a higher proportion of the ethnic minorities than of the whites choose to continue their education. For the other age groups, the difference may reflect the greater problems experienced by ethnic minority men in finding a job: economic inactivity may be a form of hidden unemployment. The differences in actual unemployment rates are discussed in Chapter 5.

Participation rates remain extremely low among Pakistani and Bangladeshi women, who are invariably Muslims: they are probably also low among Muslim women originating from India, although this cannot be shown from the LFS. The 1982 PSI survey found that a high proportion of Muslim women were looking after the home or family (78 per cent). The LFS findings suggest that this proportion may have fallen somewhat, but remains high relative to other ethnic groups. Of Bangladeshi and Pakistani women (who are mostly Muslim), 57 and 60 per cent reported that they were looking after the home or family. By contrast, participation rates remain exceptionally high among Afro-Caribbean women. Among women from other minority groups (African Asians, Africans, Indians, among whom the majority are Hindu and Sikhs, and Chinese) participation rates are about the same as for white women, or slightly lower. Afro-Caribbean women, unlike all other groups, have high participation rates regardless of whether they have dependent children. The proportion of women in part-time jobs is lower among the minority groups than among whites. Compared to 1982, the proportion of women in part-time jobs has increased from 17 to 26 per cent amongst whites, but has hardly changed amongst Afro-Caribbeans (from 17 to 16 per cent). The 1982 PSI survey gave a figure of 4 per cent for all South Asian women in part-time work. The LFS shows that the rates of part-time work remain low for Pakistani and Bangladeshi women (4 and 5 per cent), but are higher for African Asian and Indian women (15 and 13 per cent).

Table 4A   Percentage of men of working age self-employed by ethnic group, 1982 and 1988-90

Ethnic group	1982 PSI Survey	1988-90 LFS
White	9	14
Afro-Caribbean	5	9
South Asian	12	18

Self-employment is considerably more common among the Chinese, Indian and African Asian minorities than among white people. This continues a pattern already shown in 1974, and still more in 1982. Table 4A shows that the 1982 figures for self-employed males (taking all working age men as the base) were 9 per cent for whites, 5 per cent for Afro-Caribbeans and 12 per cent for South Asians (taken together). The LFS figures show a general increase in the proportions of men who are self-employed, but the former patterns remain. The rate has risen to 14 per cent among white men, to 9 per cent among Afro-Caribbean men, and to 18 per cent among South Asian men. The Afro-Caribbean self-employed are somewhat concentrated in the construction industry, whereas the South Asian self-employed are strongly concentrated in the retail sector, and in catering. One-fifth of the Pakistani self-employed have businesses in the transport and communication sector.

The distribution of dependent employees between different industry sectors is broadly similar to that found in 1982, except that there has been a continuation of the expansion of the services sector, and relative contraction of manufacturing. As in 1982, the relative growth of employment in the services sector has been faster amongst ethnic minority employees. Whilst the proportion of white male employees working in the service sector has grown from 41 to 52 per cent, the corresponding figures for Afro-Caribbean men are 45 and 59 per cent, and for African Asian men, 43 and 61 per cent. The most dramatic increase in employment in the services sector has occurred amongst Bangladeshi male employees. Whereas in 1982, only 37 per cent of them were found in services, this proportion has now risen to 75 per cent.

There has been an important change in the distribution of ethnic minorities between job levels. The proportion of Chinese, African Asian, and Indian male employees having jobs in the top category (professional, managerial, employer) is now as high as for white men, or higher. As shown by the earlier surveys, the job levels of Indian men are more polarised than those of white men: there is still a higher proportion of Indians than of whites in semi-skilled and unskilled manual jobs, but about the same proportion of Indians and whites in the top category. The same applies to the Chinese, to a greater degree. Afro-Caribbean men, as before, tend to be concentrated in skilled manual jobs, while Pakistani and Bangladeshi men still tend to be at much lower job levels than white men. A comparison of the job levels of male employees for the years 1982, 1984-86 (taken from Table 4.23), and 1988-90 shows how this situation has developed. In 1982, it was generally true that ethnic minority male employees were found at lower job levels than their white counterparts (the exception then was African Asians, of whom more were in the top category than there were of the whites). Table 4B shows how the proportions of male employees from different ethnic groups in the top SEG category then changed over the decade from 1982.

Table 4B   Percentage of male employees in top SEG category (professional, manager or employer) during the 1980s

Ethnic origin	1982 PSI Survey	1984-86 LFS	1988-90 LFS
White	19	24	27
Afro-Caribbean	5	5	12
African Asian	22	22	27
Indian	11	23	25
Pakistani	10	11	12
Bangladeshi	10	13	12

All groups now have a higher proportion of their male employees in the top category than was the case in 1982, although to very different degrees.

Male employees of Pakistani and of Bangladeshi origin have not increased their proportions in the top group by very much. Afro-Caribbeans have over doubled their representation, but from a very low base so that they still have one of the lowest proportions in the top category. African Asians have progressed steadily through the 1980s. There was a dramatic increase in the proportion of Indian male employees in the top group in the early 1980s, from 11 to 23 per cent. Most ethnic groups now have a lower proportion in the semi-skilled/unskilled manual category than was the case in 1982. The exception to this was Bangladeshi male employees, of whom about the same proportion (70 per cent) were in the bottom two categories in 1988-90 as was the case in 1982.

The groups who have the smallest representations of male employees in the top job category have all approximately doubled their proportions in the 'other non-manual' category. In 1982, the proportion of Afro-Caribbean, Pakistani and Bangladeshi men employed in such jobs was 10, 8 and 7 per cent respectively. By the end of the 1980s, these proportions had risen to 19, 16 and 14 per cent.

There has been a general increase in average job levels which has accompanied the growth in employment in the service sector. Non-manual employment has grown in both white and ethnic minority groups (taken together). Table 4C shows that the growth in importance of non-manual employment over the 1980s has been much more marked amongst ethnic minorities (from 23 per cent of employees in 1982 to 44 per cent in 1988-90). Amongst white male employees, there has been a slight growth from 42 to 47 per cent during the 1980s.

Table 4C   Percentage of male employees in non-manual jobs during the 1980s

% non-manual	1982 PSI Survey	1984-86 LFS	1988-90 LFS
White	42	44	47
Ethnic minority	23	37	43

In the case of women, the distribution across job levels is far more compressed, and the differences between ethnic groups remain fairly small, as they were in 1974 and 1982.

In 1982, of male employees qualified to A level or above, whites had distinctly better jobs than South Asians. This is no longer the case, although it is still true that well-qualified Afro-Caribbean men are in lower status jobs than men of other groups. Highly qualified men (A level or above) from all ethnic minority groups, except for Afro-Caribbeans, are now more likely to be in professional jobs than whites. Broadly speaking, among those with qualifications at a lower level, and among those with no qualifications at all, white men tend to be at higher job levels than men from ethnic minority groups. The main change since 1982, therefore, is that highly qualified men from ethnic minority groups have started to penetrate into professional and managerial jobs – especially to the professions.

While these findings about job levels of male employees constitute a substantial change from 1982, we should sound a note of caution. The classification of jobs into the five broad levels inevitably suppresses many details: sample size does not allow us to investigate these further. While non-manual employment has undoubtedly expanded more among ethnic minorities than among white employees since 1982, more detailed analysis is required of the kinds of non-manual jobs that are being done. For example, we could well find that ethnic minority men are over-represented in the marginal jobs in the service sector now, just as they tended to be confined to such jobs in manufacturing in the past. In 1982, Brown found that the ethnic differences in job levels were much more marked in manufacturing industry than in general. Table 4D shows us that this was still the case at the end of the 1980s.

Table 4D   Job levels of male employees in manufacturing industry 1988-90
(1982 PSI figures in brackets)

			Percentages
	White	Afro-Caribbean	South Asian
Professional, manager or employer	22 (13)	6 (3)	9 (5)
Other non-manual	12 (15)	8 (2)	5 (4)
Skilled manual and foremen	44 (53)	49 (52)	42 (37)
Semi-skilled or unskilled	21 (17)	37 (43)	44 (53)

(Base: all male employees in engineering, vehicles, shipbuilding; other manufacturing; and mining)

Table 4E shows the job levels of male employees in the service sector.[12] The disparity between ethnic groups is still substantially less than in manufacturing industry. South Asian men (taken together) now have a similar proportion of their employees in the top category to that of white men. Afro-Caribbean men have substantially fewer in the top category than either of the other groups, but have closed the gap somewhat since 1982.

Thus, the relative decline of employment in the manufacturing sector and the simultaneous expansion of the service sector will manifest themselves in an improvement in the average job levels of ethnic minority men, as the sector in which they fare worst is contracting.

On three measures of mobility – in and out of the labour market, between employers, and between jobs – differences between ethnic groups were rather small, although job mobility was distinctly lower among Pakistani and Bangladeshi men than among whites.

As in 1974 and 1982, a much higher proportion of Pakistanis than of whites were working shifts. Shiftwork was also slightly more common among other ethnic minority groups than among whites. A more detailed analysis suggests that younger people belonging to ethnic minority groups are not following the older generation into jobs that involve shiftwork.

Table 4E   Job levels of male employees in service industries 1988-90 (1982 PSI figures in brackets)

			Percentages
	White	Afro-Caribbean	South Asian
Professional, manager, or employer	32 (26)	14 (6)	31 (23)
Other non-manual	25 (28)	26 (18)	30 (26)
Skilled manual and foremen	24 (33)	34 (45)	17 (26)
Semi-skilled and unskilled manual	18 (13)	25 (31)	21 (22)

The earlier surveys found that trade union membership rates were higher among Afro-Caribbeans and South Asians than among whites, even after controlling for job level. The substantial changes in industrial structure and employment legislation over the past ten years have led to a considerable reduction in trade union membership overall, as is shown in Table 4F. The 1982 survey found that of white male employees, 57 per cent were trade union members. This compared with 64 per cent of Afro-Caribbean male employees and 59 per cent of South Asians. The rates for white and Afro-Caribbean men had by 1988-90 dropped to 40 and 48 per cent respectively. It is difficult to compare change in the South Asian rate because the 1982 figures combine what are clearly very different groups. Indians have a slightly higher rate than whites, Pakistanis and

African Asians a somewhat lower rate, and Bangladeshi male employees have (at 12 per cent) the lowest union membership rate of all the groups studied. In short, rates of membership remain higher among Afro-Caribbeans than among whites, but they are now about the same among Indians and Pakistanis as among whites, and much lower among Bangladeshis and Chinese people. These patterns remain much the same when the analysis is carried out within age groups and job levels. However, for all ethnic groups rates of membership are substantially higher among older than among younger age groups.

Table 4F   Percentage of male employees members of trade unions by ethnic group, 1982 and 1988-90

Ethnic group	1982 PSI Survey	1988-90 LFS
White	57	38
Afro-Caribbean	64	47
South Asian	59	36

Dual labour market theory asserts that in the secondary sector of the labour market jobs are often temporary, seasonal, or part-time, tend to be low-paid, and offer little prospect of training or advancement. Using a rough definition of the secondary sector (the best that can be done with the LFS data) only one of the ethnic minority groups (Bangladeshis) is markedly concentrated there; the proportions of the other ethnic minority groups that are within the secondary sector are either about the same as for whites, or lower.

The earnings achieved are a central part of the labour market experience of any individual. Earlier studies found that racial disadvantage was to a large extent reflected in relative earnings. The lack of recent information about the earnings of ethnic minorities is an important gap in knowledge about their relative labour market position. Information of that kind, which can best be provided by a national survey of ethnic minorities, is essential in order to place in context the important changes so far shown by analysis of the Labour Force Survey.[13]

Notes
1. But the differences are at the borderline of statistical significance.
2. David Drew, John Gray and Nicholas Sime, *Against the Odds: the Education and Labour Market Experiences of Black Young People*, Youth Cohort Study: England and Wales: Department of Employment, 1992.
3. The definitions of full and part-time jobs are based on self-report in the LFS.
4. This material is summarised in C. Brown, *Racial Inequality in the British Labour Market*, Employment Institute, Economic Report, 5.4, June 1990.
5. M. Corcoran and G. Duncan, 'Work history, labour force attachment and earnings: differences between races and sexes', *Journal of Human Resources* 14:1, 1979.
6. M. Stewart, 'Racial discrimination and occupational attainment in Britain', *Economic Journal* 93:371, 1983.
7. See, for example, B. Chiswick, 'The earnings of white and coloured male immigrants in Britain', *Economica* 47:185, 1980.
8. P. J. Dolton, G. H. Makepeace and G. D. Inchley, *The Early Careers of 1980 graduates: Earnings, earnings differentials and post-graduate study*, Employment Department research paper 78, 1990.
9. B. McCormick, 'Evidence about the comparative earnings of Asian and West Indian workers in Great Britain', *Scottish Journal of Political Economy*, 33:2, 1986.
10. *Earnings and ethnicity*, Leicester City Council, 1990.
11. This survey asked respondents to indicate their ethnic origins. Although a wide variety of responses were allowed they were aggregated in the analysis into whites and Non-whites. Whereas the estimates for whites are based on a sample of nearly 5,000 people, those for non-whites are based on a sample of 108.
12. The LFS analysis uses the same definition of the service sector as was used in the *Black and White Britain* report. This includes all employees in industry divisions 6, 7, 8, and 9, but does not include those working in public administration and defence.
13. It is intended that the LFS will include a question on earnings in future years.

Percentages

Table 4.1 Labour force participation rates by ethnic group, age and sex (all working age), 1988-90

	Age 16-59/64 All working age			Age 16-24			Age 25-44			Age 45-59/64		
	All	M	F	All	M	F	All	M	F	All	M	F
All origins	80	89	71	79	84	73	84	96	72	75	81	66
White	81	89	71	80	86	74	85	97	73	75	81	67
Total ethnic minority	70	81	57	58	65	52	74	90	59	74	83	60
Afro-Caribbean	81	85	76	74	78	70	83	91	76	83	84	83
African Asian	79	89	69	61	62	60	87	98	75	76	90	58
Indian	71	84	57	57	64	50	79	95	63	71	84	52
Pakistani	51	77	23	44	55	34	53	90	19	59	81	13
Bangladeshi	52	79	23	53	77	31	53	89	22	50	70	*
Chinese	65	75	55	43	49	37	69	80	59	78	87	62
African	67	72	61	57	60	54	67	74	60	80	81	78
Other/Mixed	70	78	61	58	64	53	75	85	63	76	82	69

Source: 1988, 1989, 1990 Labour Force Surveys (GB)

* Sample size too small

Table 4.2 Economic activity rates of women, by marital status, dependent children and ethnic group, 1988-90

	Married/Cohabiting			Single		
	All	With children	Without children	All	With children[+]	Without children[+]
All origins	69	63	76	74	58	81
White	70	64	76	74	59	81
Total ethnic minority	56	49	70	60	48	70
Afro-Caribbean	80	74	87	73	59	85
African Asian	70	69	74	64	*	72
Indian	59	57	63	53	42	61
Pakistani	19	17	31	36	36	36
Bangladeshi	18	14	*	39	*	*
Chinese	58	52	70	47	*	55
African	66	62	75	55	46	63
Other/Mixed	62	54	76	59	49	68

Source: 1988, 1989, 1990 Labour Force Surveys (GB)

*   Sample size too small

[+]   Dependent children aged under 16

Column Percentages

Table 4.3 Economic status of people aged 16-24 by ethnic group, 1988-90

	All origins	White	Total ethnic minority	Afro-Caribbean	African Asian	Indian	Pakistani	Bangla-deshi	Chinese	African	Other/Mixed
All Persons											
Economically Active	79	80	58	74	61	57	44	53	43	57	58
of which: in Employment	70	72	47	57	53	48	31	43	40	42	51
Employee	61	63	40	50	47	40	22	35	38	40	46
Self Employed	5	4	3	2	5	5	4	3	1	0	2
On Government Scheme	5	5	3	4	2	3	5	5	1	2	3
Labour Force Unemployed	9	8	11	17	7	9	13	10	3	15	7
Economically Inactive	21	20	42	26	39	43	56	47	57	43	42
of which: Full time Student	13	12	29	16	29	33	33	24	53	36	32
Looking After Family/Home	6	6	8	6	7	7	17	18	2	5	6
Men 16-24											
Economically Active	84	86	65	78	62	64	55	77	49	60	64
of which: in Employment	74	76	52	59	56	52	38	66	44	43	54
Employee	62	64	43	50	45	41	29	59	43	41	49
Self Employed	6	6	5	3	8	8	5	6	1	0	2
On Government Scheme	6	6	4	6	4	4	5	0	0	2	3
Labour Force Unemployed	10	10	13	19	6	12	17	11	5	17	9
Economically Inactive	16	14	35	22	38	36	45	23	51	40	36
of which: Full time Student	14	13	32	16	38	33	40	21	49	36	33
Women 16-24											
Economically Active	73	74	52	70	60	50	34	31	37	54	53
of which: in Employment	66	67	42	54	51	44	24	22	36	40	47
Employee	60	62	37	50	48	39	16	12	33	38	43
Self Employed	2	2	2	1	1	3	2	0	1	2	1
On Government Scheme	4	4	3	3	1	2	5	10	1	2	3
Labour Force Unemployed	7	7	10	16	9	6	10	9	1	14	6
Economically Inactive	27	26	48	30	40	50	66	69	63	46	47
of which: Full time Student	13	12	27	16	21	32	26	26	57	36	30
Looking After Family/Home	12	12	17	11	15	14	33	35	4	10	12

Source: 1988, 1989, 1990 Labour Force Surveys (GB)

Table 4.4   Economic status of all people of working age by ethnic group, 1988-90

Column Percentages

	All origins	White	Total ethnic minority	Afro-Caribbean	African Asian	Indian	Pakistani	Bangla-deshi	Chinese	African	Other/Mixed
All persons of working age											
Economically Active	80	81	70	81	79	71	51	52	65	67	70
of which: in Employment	74	75	60	69	72	63	40	40	60	57	63
Employee (excl. Gov't scheme)	63	64	49	61	58	48	28	30	42	52	54
Full-time	50	50	41	52	49	41	24	26	33	41	44
Part-time	13	14	8	9	8	7	4	5	9	11	10
Self-Employed	9	9	10	6	14	13	9	7	18	4	8
Employed on Government Scheme	1	1	2	2	1	1	2	3	0	1	2
YTS - employer based	1	1	0	0	0	0	1	0	0	0	0
YTS - college based	0	0	0	0	0	0	0	1	0	0	0
Other government schemes	1	1	1	2	1	1	1	2	0	1	1
Unemployed	6	6	9	12	7	8	11	12	5	9	7
Economically Inactive	20	19	30	19	21	29	49	48	35	33	30
of which: Full-time Students	3	3	10	6	7	9	11	10	17	17	13
Looking after Family/Home	9	8	13	6	10	12	29	28	12	9	11

Contd

Table 4.4   Economic status of all people of working age by ethnic group, 1988-90 (Contd)

Column Percentages

	All origins	White	Total ethnic minority	Afro-Caribbean	African Asian	Indian	Pakistani	Bangla-deshi	Chinese	African	Other/Mixed
Men											
Economically Active	89	89	81	85	89	84	77	79	75	72	78
of which: in Employment	82	82	70	72	82	74	60	60	68	62	71
Employee (excl. Gov't scheme)	66	67	54	60	61	53	44	46	44	53	58
Full-time	64	64	51	58	58	51	40	42	39	49	54
Part-time	2	2	3	2	2	2	4	4	5	5	4
Self-Employed	14	14	15	9	20	20	15	13	24	7	12
Employed on Government Scheme	2	2	2	3	1	1	2	1	0	1	2
YTS - employer based	1	1	0	1	0	1	0	0	0	0	0
YTS - college based	0	0	0	0	0	0	1	0	0	0	0
Other government schemes	1	1	1	2	1	1	1	1	0	1	1
Unemployed	7	7	11	13	7	10	17	19	7	10	7
Economically Inactive	11	11	19	15	11	16	23	21	25	28	22
of which: Full-time Students	3	3	11	6	9	9	13	9	20	21	15
Looking after Family/Home	0	0	0	1	0	0	1	1	0	0	1

Contd

Table 4.4   Economic status of all people of working age by ethnic group, 1988-90 (Contd)

Column Percentages

Women	All origins	White	Total ethnic minority	Afro-Caribbean	African Asian	Indian	Pakistani	Bangla-deshi	Chinese	African	Other/Mixed
Economically Active	71	71	57	76	69	57	23	23	55	61	61
of which: in Employment	65	66	50	66	62	50	17	18	53	53	54
Employee (excl. Gov't scheme)	60	61	44	62	54	44	12	12	41	50	49
Full-time	34	35	31	46	40	31	8	7	27	33	33
Part-time	25	26	13	16	15	13	4	5	14	17	16
Self-Employed	5	5	4	2	6	6	4	1	12	2	4
Employed on Government Scheme	1	1	1	2	1	1	2	5	0	1	2
YTS - employer based	1	1	0	0	0	0	1	1	0	0	0
YTS - college based	0	0	0	0	0	0	0	1	0	0	0
Other government schemes	0	0	1	2	1	1	1	3	0	1	1
Unemployed	5	5	7	10	7	7	6	5	2	8	7
Economically Inactive	29	29	43	24	31	43	77	77	45	39	39
of which: Full-time Students	3	3	9	5	5	9	9	11	4	14	9
Looking after Family/Home	18	17	27	12	20	25	60	57	25	19	22

Source: 1988, 1989, 1990 Labour Force Surveys (GB)

Table 4.5   Industry distribution by ethnic group, all self-employed, 1988-90

Column Percentages

	All origins	White	Total ethnic minority	Afro-Caribbean	African Asian	Indian	Pakistani	Bangla-deshi	Chinese	African	Other/Mixed
0 Agriculture, forestry and fishing	8	9	0	1	0	0	0	*	1	*	0
1 Energy and water supply	0	0	0	0	1	0	0	*	0	*	0
2 Extraction minerals, metal manufacture	1	1	0	1	0	0	0	*	0	*	1
3 Metal goods, engineering and vehicles	3	3	1	1	1	2	1	*	0	*	3
Motor vehicles and parts	0	0	0	0	0	0	0	*	0	*	0
4 Other manufacturing	6	6	5	5	4	4	7	*	1	*	3
Textiles	0	0	0	1	0	0	0	*	0	*	0
Clothing and footwear	1	1	3	2	4	3	5	*	0	*	0
5 Construction	23	24	9	34	4	8	5	*	0	*	13
6 Distribution, hotels, catering and repairs	25	23	56	19	72	62	53	*	86	*	33
Retail distribution	14	13	36	9	58	51	46	*	9	*	16
Hotels and catering	5	5	14	3	4	5	4	*	75	*	11
7 Transport and communications	5	5	6	8	2	2	20	*	2	*	3
8 Banking and finance	12	12	10	9	11	10	9	*	2	*	14
9 Other services	17	17	13	23	5	11	6	*	9	*	31
Public administration, defence etc	0	0	0	0	1	0	0	*	1	*	2
Education	2	2	1	3	0	1	0	*	0	*	1
Hospitals, medical care institutions	0	0	1	1	1	0	0	*	2	*	0

Source: 1988, 1989, 1990 Labour Force Surveys (GB)

* Sample size too small

Table 4.6 Self-employed with or without staff by ethnic group, 1988-90

Column Percentages

	All origins	White	Total ethnic minority	Afro-Caribbean	African Asian	Indian	Pakistani	Bangla-deshi	Chinese	African	Other/Mixed
Without employees	68	69	61	82	55	60	65	33	38	89	63
With employees	32	31	39	17	45	39	35	67	62	11	37
Less than 25 employees	30	29	37	17	43	39	33	67	60	9	33
25+ employees	2	2	1	0	2	0	2	0	2	2	3

Source: 1988, 1989, 1990 Labour Force Surveys (GB)

Table 4.7   Industry distribution by ethnic group, all employees, 1988-90

Column Percentages

	All origins	White	Total ethnic minority	Afro-Caribbean	African Asian	Indian	Pakistani	Bangla-deshi	Chinese	African	Other/Mixed
0 Agriculture, forestry and fishing	**1**	**1**	**0**	**0**	**0**	**0**	**0**	**0**	**0**	**0**	**0**
1 Energy and water supply	**3**	**3**	**1**	**1**	**2**	**1**	**0**	**0**	**0**	**1**	**1**
2 Extraction minerals, metal manufacture	**4**	**4**	**2**	**2**	**3**	**3**	**5**	**2**	**1**	**1**	**2**
3 Metal goods, engineering and vehicles	**11**	**11**	**12**	**12**	**14**	**16**	**16**	**5**	**5**	**8**	**8**
Motor vehicles and parts	2	2	3	3	3	4	6	2	0	1	1
4 Other manufacturing	**10**	**10**	**13**	**9**	**13**	**19**	**32**	**15**	**4**	**5**	**7**
Textiles	1	1	2	1	4	4	11	0	0	1	0
Clothing and footwear	1	1	3	1	2	6	6	12	2	2	1
5 Construction	**5**	**5**	**3**	**4**	**3**	**2**	**2**	**1**	**0**	**2**	**3**
6 Distribution, hotels, catering and repairs	**20**	**20**	**22**	**15**	**24**	**19**	**19**	**47**	**47**	**20**	**25**
Retail distribution	11	11	11	8	18	11	11	6	7	10	12
Hotels and catering	4	4	7	4	2	4	5	41	38	8	8
7 Transport and communication	**6**	**6**	**8**	**10**	**10**	**8**	**8**	**2**	**4**	**8**	**7**
8 Banking and finance etc	**11**	**11**	**11**	**11**	**15**	**10**	**7**	**6**	**10**	**11**	**13**
Business services	5	5	5	5	7	5	2	2	5	6	7
9 Other services	**29**	**29**	**28**	**36**	**16**	**21**	**11**	**23**	**29**	**45**	**35**
Public administration, defence etc	7	7	5	6	6	4	3	6	4	10	6
Education	8	8	4	5	3	3	2	6	3	6	6
Hospitals, medical care institutions	5	5	9	13	4	7	2	3	13	14	11

Source: 1988, 1989, 1990 Labour Force Surveys (GB)

Table 4.8   Industry distribution by ethnic group, all male employees, 1988-90

Column Percentages

	All origins	White	Total ethnic minority	Afro-Caribbean	African Asian	Indian	Pakistani	Bangla-deshi	Chinese	African	Other/Mixed
0 Agriculture, forestry and fishing	**2**	**2**	**0**	**0**	**0**	**0**	**0**	**1**	**0**	**0**	**0**
1 Energy and water supply	**4**	**4**	**1**	**1**	**2**	**1**	**0**	**0**	**1**	**0**	**2**
2 Extraction minerals, metal manufacture	**5**	**5**	**3**	**3**	**3**	**4**	**5**	**2**	**0**	**1**	**3**
3 Metal goods, engineering and vehicles	**16**	**16**	**16**	**18**	**17**	**22**	**18**	**3**	**9**	**10**	**10**
Motor vehicles and parts	3	3	5	5	4	6	7	3	1	3	2
4 Other manufacturing	**11**	**11**	**14**	**12**	**13**	**18**	**32**	**18**	**5**	**6**	**7**
Textiles	1	1	3	1	4	3	12	0	0	1	0
Clothing and footwear	1	1	2	0	1	3	2	15	3	1	1
5 Construction	**8**	**9**	**4**	**6**	**5**	**3**	**3**	**1**	**1**	**2**	**5**
6 Distribution, hotels, catering and repairs	**16**	**15**	**22**	**16**	**24**	**17**	**15**	**53**	**53**	**20**	**25**
Retail distribution	8	8	10	10	17	8	8	3	7	11	11
Hotels and catering	2	2	7	3	2	3	4	50	43	6	9
7 Transport and communication	**9**	**9**	**12**	**17**	**11**	**12**	**10**	**2**	**4**	**13**	**8**
8 Banking and finance etc	**9**	**9**	**10**	**9**	**14**	**8**	**7**	**6**	**9**	**11**	**13**
Business services	5	5	5	5	8	5	2	3	6	6	7
9 Other services	**19**	**19**	**18**	**17**	**12**	**16**	**9**	**14**	**19**	**37**	**27**
Public administration, defence etc	7	8	5	5	4	4	2	3	5	10	5
Education	5	5	3	2	2	2	2	4	2	5	5
Hospitals, medical care institutions	2	2	5	4	2	6	2	2	7	7	7

Source: 1988, 1989, 1990 Labour Force Surveys (GB)

Table 4.9 Industry distribution by ethnic group, all female employees, 1988-90

Column Percentages

	All origins	White	Total ethnic minority	Afro-Caribbean	African Asian	Indian	Pakistani	Bangladeshi	Chinese	African	Other/Mixed
0 Agriculture, forestry and fishing	1	1	0	0	0	0	1	*	0	0	0
1 Energy and water supply	1	1	1	1	2	0	0	*	0	1	0
2 Extraction minerals, metal manufacture	2	2	1	1	2	1	1	*	1	2	1
3 Metal goods, engineering and vehicles	5	5	7	6	11	8	9	*	1	6	5
Motor vehicles and parts	0	0	1	0	1	2	1	*	0	0	0
4 Other manufacturing	9	8	12	7	14	22	33	*	4	4	6
Textiles	1	1	2	0	4	5	4	*	0	0	1
Clothing and footwear	2	2	5	3	4	9	22	*	2	3	1
5 Construction	2	2	1	1	0	0	0	*	0	1	2
6 Distribution, hotels, catering and repairs	25	25	22	14	24	22	33	*	41	20	25
Retail distribution	15	15	12	7	18	14	23	*	7	8	14
Hotels and catering	7	7	7	5	1	5	7	*	33	10	7
7 Transport and communication	3	3	4	4	8	4	0	*	4	2	4
8 Banking and finance etc	12	12	12	12	17	13	4	*	10	11	12
Business services	6	6	6	6	5	7	1	*	5	6	6
9 Other services	41	41	40	55	21	28	20	*	39	53	44
Public administration, defence etc	6	6	6	6	7	5	6	*	3	10	8
Education	12	12	6	8	4	5	4	*	5	7	7
Hospitals, medical care institutions	9	8	15	22	6	9	3	*	19	22	15

Source: 1988, 1989, 1990 Labour Force Surveys (GB)

*Sample size too small

Table 4.10 Job levels of male employees by ethnic group, 1988-90

Column Percentages

	All origins	White	Total ethnic minority	Afro-Caribbean	African Asian	Indian	Pakistani	Bangla-deshi	Chinese	African	Other/Mixed
Prof/Manager/Employer	27	27	21	12	27	25	12	12	30	21	30
Employees & Managers - large establishments	13	13	7	5	6	9	4	1	7	9	11
Employees & Managers - small establishments	7	7	5	3	10	5	4	5	10	3	7
Professional workers - employees	7	7	8	4	11	10	4	6	14	9	12
Other non-manual	20	20	22	19	30	18	16	14	19	34	31
Skilled manual & Foremen	32	33	28	39	26	29	34	5	10	20	18
Semi-skilled manual	15	15	23	23	13	24	31	65	36	18	16
Unskilled manual	4	4	5	6	3	4	6	5	4	4	2
Armed Services/inadequately described/not stated	1	1	1	1	0	0	1	0	1	3	3

Source: 1988, 1989, 1990 Labour Force Surveys (GB)

Table 4.11 Job levels of female employees by ethnic group, 1988-90

Column Percentages

	All origins	White	Total ethnic minority	Afro-Caribbean	African Asian	Indian	Pakistani	Bangla-deshi	Chinese	African	Other/Mixed
Prof/Manager/Employer	11	11	9	8	7	10	4	*	16	11	12
Employees and Managers - large establishments	6	6	4	5	3	4	1	*	4	5	4
Employees & Managers - small establishments	4	4	3	2	2	2	3	*	5	3	4
Professional workers - employees	2	2	2	1	2	4	0	*	7	2	3
Other non-manual	55	56	53	54	58	47	42	*	53	47	63
Skilled manual & Foremen	5	5	5	4	9	5	7	*	2	6	3
Semi-skilled manual	22	22	27	25	25	34	45	*	20	32	17
Unskilled manual	7	7	5	9	1	4	2	*	9	4	5
Armed services/inadequately described/not stated	0	0	0	0	0	0	0	*	0	1	0

Source: 1988, 1989, 1990 Labour Force Surveys (GB)

* Sample size too small

Table 4.12 Job levels of male employees by highest qualification and ethnic group, 1988-90

	All origins	White	Total ethnic minority	Afro-Caribbean	African Asian	Indian	Pakistani	Bangla-deshi	Chinese	African	Other/Mixed
Percentage in professional/ manager/employer category (prof workers in brackets)											
A-Level or higher	37(12)	37(12)	37(18)	23(8)	42(23)	45(21)	30(14)	*	48(29)	30(13)	44(22)
O-Level/CSE/Other	21(2)	21(2)	14(2)	7(1)	19(1)	16(5)	12(2)	*	*	*	19(4)
No qualification	11(1)	11(1)	5(1)	3(0)	8(1)	5(1)	4(0)	3(0)	*	*	8(0)
% in other non-manual category											
A-Level or higher	22	22	27	23	29	22	34	*	25	34	32
O-Level/CSE/Other	25	25	30	31	41	23	21	*	*	*	37
No qualification	11	11	9	5	19	8	7	4	*	*	16
% in skilled manual category											
A-Level or higher	30	31	24	39	23	22	30	*	7	20	14
O-Level/CSE/Other	31	31	26	34	22	30	40	*	*	*	17
No qualification	38	39	34	42	40	38	33	5	*	*	31
% in semi-skilled manual category											
A-Level or higher	8	8	10	13	6	9	5	*	18	11	8
O-Level/CSE/Other	17	17	22	22	15	27	23	*	*	*	18
No qualification	29	28	42	35	26	40	47	50	*	*	34
% in unskilled manual category											
A-Level or higher	1	1	1	1	0	1	1	*	1	3	1
O-Level/CSE/Other	4	4	4	5	4	4	3	*	*	*	2
No qualification	11	11	10	15	8	9	10	7	*	*	7

Source: 1988, 1989, 1990 Labour Force Surveys (GB)

*   Sample size too small

Table 4.13 Job levels of female employees by highest qualification and ethnic group,1988-90

	All origins	White	Total ethnic minority	Afro-Caribbean	African Asian	Indian	Pakistani	Bangla-deshi	Chinese	African	Other/Mixed
Percentage in professional/ manager/employer category (prof workers in brackets)											
A-Level or higher	22 (5)	23 (5)	19 (6)	16 (2)	14 (5)	25 (11)	*	*	28 (15)	21 (4)	22 (8)
O-Level/CSE/Other	9	9	6	7	6	5	*	*	*	4	8
No qualification	4	5	2	1	1	1	*	*	*	*	1
% in other non-manual category											
A-Level or higher	61	61	66	67	72	65	*	*	60	56	69
O-Level/CSE/Other	67	67	66	68	67	65	*	*	*	53	72
No qualification	37	37	23	21	28	16	*	*	*	*	38
% in skilled manual category											
A-Level or higher	3	3	2	1	4	1	*	*	2	4	2
O-Level/CSE/Other	4	4	3	3	4	4	*	*	*	4	2
No qualification	8	8	9	8	21	8	*	*	*	*	5
% in semi-skilled manual category											
A-Level or higher	12	12	11	14	10	9	*	*	9	18	6
O-Level/CSE/Other	17	17	22	18	22	24	*	*	*	34	16
No qualification	36	36	52	46	46	68	*	*	*	*	40
% in unskilled manual category											
A-Level or higher	1	1	1	1	0	1	*	*	2	2	1
O-Level/CSE/Other	3	3	3	4	1	2	*	*	*	5	3
No qualification	15	15	13	23	4	7	*	*	*	*	15

Source: 1988, 1989, 1990 Labour Force Surveys (GB)

* Sample size too small

Table 4.14 Job levels of qualified male ethnic minority employees by where gained highest qualification, 1988-90

Column Percentages

	Total ethnic minority	Afro-Caribbean	African Asian	Indian	Pakistani	Bangla-deshi	Chinese	African	Other/Mixed	All white male employees with qualif.
Qualified UK										
Professional/Manager/Employer	26	17	36	33	17	*	43	18	30	32
Other Non-Manual	31	31	32	24	33	*	24	40	36	23
Skilled Manual and Foreman	25	33	23	25	36	*	8	20	19	31
Semi-skilled Manual	15	16	8	16	10	*	18	19	13	11
Unskilled Manual	2	2	1	2	3	*	6	4	1	3
Qualified Abroad										
Professional/Manager/Employer	30	13	26	36	21	*	*	27	41	
Other Non-Manual	25	13	38	20	19	*	*	31	32	
Skilled Manual and Foreman	24	50	19	26	34	*	*	21	8	
Semi-skilled Manual	16	18	13	15	24	*	*	13	12	
Unskilled Manual	2	3	3	2	2	*	*	2	1	

Source: 1988, 1989, 1990 Labour Force Surveys (GB)

* Sample size too small

Table 4.15 Mobility between employers by ethnic group (employees aged 25-44), 1988-90

	All origins	White	Total ethnic minority	Afro-Caribbean	African Asian	Indian	Pakistani	Bangla-deshi	Chinese	African	Other/Mixed
% working for a different employer from a year ago											
All	13	13	15	16	13	13	11	19	18	19	16
Men	13	12	15	17	13	12	12	20	19	20	16
Women	14	14	14	15	13	14	10	*	16	19	15

Source: 1988, 1989, 1990 Labour Force Surveys (GB)

* Sample size too small

Table 4.16 Job mobility by ethnic group (employees aged 25-44), 1988-90

	All origins	White	Total ethnic minority	Afro-Caribbean	African Asian	Indian	Pakistani	Bangla-deshi	Chinese	African	Other/Mixed
% working in a different job from a year ago											
All	15	15	13	16	13	11	10	7	13	15	16
Men	14	14	13	14	14	11	9	5	10	17	17
Women	16	16	14	18	12	11	12	*	17	13	14

Source: 1988, 1989, 1990 Labour Force Surveys (GB)

* Sample size too small

Table 4.17 Mean (average) actual weekly hours worked by employees of different ethnic groups, 1988-90

	All origins	White	Total ethnic minority	Afro-Caribbean	African Asian	Indian	Pakistani	Bangla-deshi	Chinese	African	Other/Mixed
Men											
Full-time	43.0	43.0	42.6	41.3	43.2	42.6	44.0	43.6	44.5	41.8	42.5
Part-time	15.2	15.2	15.4	15.6	13.5	14.2	16.0	13.3	17.6	18.0	14.8
Women											
Full-time	37.6	37.5	38.0	37.0	38.0	38.7	39.5	38.0	41.9	37.4	37.5
Part-time	17.1	17.0	19.4	20.1	21.0	19.4	15.7	10.3	17.1	22.0	18.6

Source: 1988, 1989, 1990 Labour Force Surveys (GB)

105

Table 4.18 Percentage of employees doing shifts by ethnic group (all working age), 1988-90

Percentages

	Age 16-59/64 All working age			Age 16-24			Age 25-44			Age 45-59/64		
	All	M	F	All	M	F	All	M	F	All	M	F
All origins	15	18	11	13	15	12	16	20	12	14	18	10
White	15	18	11	13	15	12	16	20	11	14	17	9
Total ethnic minority	20	26	13	11	13	9	21	27	14	27	33	16
Afro-Caribbean	22	26	19	13	12	13	20	21	19	32	40	23
African Asian	14	20	6	8	11	5	15	22	6	15	21	*
Indian	20	28	9	9	13	6	22	33	10	23	28	12
Pakistani	33	40	4	17	22	*	35	43	*	45	48	*
Bangladeshi	18	22	*	15	*	*	*	*	*	*	*	*
Chinese	16	14	18	9	*	*	21	18	23	10	*	*
African	19	23	15	12	*	*	22	27	16	19	20	*
Mixed/Other	17	20	13	9	10	8	20	23	16	21	28	13

Source: 1988, 1989, 1990 Labour Force Surveys (GB)

* Sample size too small

Table 4.19 Number of employees at workplace by ethnic group (all employees), 1988-90

	All origins	White	Total ethnic minority	Afro-Caribbean	African Asian	Indian	Pakistani	Bangla-deshi	Chinese	African	Other/Mixed
Percentage with less than 25 employees	33	33	29	25	29	26	28	66	53	25	31
Percentage with 25 or more employees	67	67	71	74	71	74	72	34	47	75	69

Source: 1988, 1989, 1990 Labour Force Surveys (GB)

Table 4.20 Trade union membership rates by ethnic group, sex and age, 1989-90 (employees)

Percentages

	Age 16-59/64 All working age			Age 16-24			Age 25-44			Age 45-59/64		
	All	M	F	All	M	F	All	M	F	All	M	F
All origins	35	39	29	21	23	20	36	41	30	42	48	34
White	35	40	29	22	23	20	36	42	30	42	47	34
Total Ethnic Minority	34	35	31	16	13	19	34	36	32	49	52	43
Afro-Caribbean	44	48	41	21	20	22	43	45	41	63	69	55
African Asian	28	32	23	16	*	*	30	35	24	31	*	*
Indian	38	42	32	18	14	22	41	48	33	46	50	38
Pakistani	33	36	19	16	*	*	36	39	*	40	42	*
Bangladeshi	14	12	*	6	*	*	*	*	*	*	*	*
Chinese	19	15	22	*	*	*	18	13	23	*	*	*
African	31	28	33	13	*	*	27	22	31	56	*	*
Other/Mixed	25	24	25	12	12	11	26	23	31	37	47	*

Source: 1989, 1990 Labour Force Surveys (GB)

* Sample size too small

Table 4.21   Trade union membership rate by job level and ethnic group (all employees), 1989-90

Percentages

Job level	Professional/ Manager/ Employer	Other Non- Manual	Skilled Manual	Semi- skilled Manual	Unskilled Manual
All origins	26	31	50	37	32
White	26	31	50	37	32
Total Ethnic Minority	25	31	49	34	31
Afro-Caribbean	42	39	57	46	33
African Asian	13	24	45	32	*
Indian	26	36	48	39	*
Pakistani	*	23	49	32	*
Bangladeshi	*	*	*	9	*
Chinese	17	31	*	4	*
African	39	28	*	31	*
Other/Mixed	20	25	40	25	*

Source: 1989, 1990 Labour Force Surveys (GB)

*   Sample size too small

Table 4.22 Percentage of employees working in the secondary sector by ethnic group, 1988-90

	All origins	White	Total ethnic minority	Afro-Caribbean	African Asian	Indian	Pakistani	Bangla-deshi	Chinese	African	Other/Mixed
Secondary sector[+]	53	53	52	44	53	53	63	80	66	43	53

Source: 1988, 1989, 1990 Labour Force Surveys (GB)

+ The secondary sector is here defined as the other manufacturing and distribution, repairs, hotels and catering sectors; the small firm (less than 25 employees) sector; temporary, seasonal or casual jobs; fixed period jobs.

Table 4.23 Job levels of male employees by ethnic group, 1984-86

Column percentages

	All origins	White	Total ethnic minority	Afro-Caribbean	African Asian	Indian	Pakistani	Bangla-deshi	Chinese	African	Other/Mixed
Prof/Manager/Employer	24	24	18	5	22	23	11	13	31	18	30
Employers & Managers-large establishments	11	11	5	2	4	6	1	1	4	6	11
Employers & Managers-small establishments	6	6	4	1	5	5	5	5	9	3	6
Professional workers-employees	7	7	9	2	13	12	4	7	19	9	13
Other non-manual	20	20	19	15	23	21	12	9	18	40	21
Skilled manual & Foremen	34	34	31	45	30	29	39	16	9	17	21
Semi-skilled manual	16	15	24	23	20	21	32	56	39	21	19
Unskilled manual	5	5	6	10	3	5	6	6	3	1	3
Armed services/inadequately described/not stated	1	1	1	1	0	0	0	0	0	3	5

Source:1984,1985,1986 Labour Force Surveys (GB)

5 Unemployment

During the boom years of the 1950s, the then largely immigrant population of ethnic minority workers, like the indigenous population, suffered low rates and only short spells of unemployment. However, as the UK economy was increasingly characterised by high rates of unemployment, it became clear that ethnic minority workers were much more vulnerable than white workers to changes in the economic climate. There is strong evidence that ethnic minority unemployment is 'hyper-cyclical'.[1] This means that when the economy is contracting, ethnic minority unemployment rises much faster and to a higher peak, than does white unemployment. Similarly, when the economy begins to expand, unemployment amongst ethnic minorities falls at a higher rate than among white people. Thus, during the period of the late 1980s when the overall unemployment rate was falling, we would expect to find a narrowing of the gap between ethnic minority and white unemployment rates. As unemployment has been rising in the early 1990s, this gap is likely to be opening up again.

A number of studies have shown that unemployment was higher among ethnic minorities than among white people.[2] This chapter will examine whether this pattern has continued over the 1980s, and look at possible explanations for higher rates amongst minority groups, such as type of occupation and level of qualification.

Unemployment rates

The LFS uses the International Labour Organisation's definition of unemployment. That is, a person is classified as unemployed if, in the week before the survey he or she did not have a paid job, had actively sought work at some time during the last four weeks, and was available to start work within the next fortnight.

Table 5.1 clearly shows that white people are still much less prone to unemployment than ethnic minorities. Compared to a white rate of 7 per cent for 1988-90, the overall rate amongst ethnic minorities was 13 per cent. Unemployment is higher amongst men and people aged 16-24 than among women and the older age groups. The overall figures hide substantial differences within the ethnic minority population. There is a marked division in the circumstances of different groups within the South Asian population. Whilst African Asians and Indians have unemployment rates closest to that of the white population, people of Pakistani and Bangladeshi origin suffer from higher rates of unemployment than any other racial group. The Afro-Caribbean rate is higher than that of Indians and African Asians, but not as high as for Pakistanis or Bangladeshis.

Among those aged 16-24 these differences are magnified. Young Pakistanis have a particularly high unemployment rate, which at 30 per cent is about three times the rate for young whites. The rate for young people of African origin is nearly as high (27 per cent), and that for young Afro-Caribbeans (23 per cent) is over double the white rate. The lowest rate of unemployment in this age group is found among African Asian men, who with a rate of just 9 per cent have a similar likelihood to young white men of being unemployed.

In the 25-44 age group, people of white and African Asian origin have the same unemployment rates – at 7 per cent the lowest for any ethnic group. In general, the differences between ethnic groups are smaller in this age group, but much higher rates for people of Pakistani and Bangladeshi origin still stand out (18 and 23 per cent respectively). In the pre-retirement age group, the same general pattern applies: the white unemployment rate (6 per cent) is substantially lower than that of all other ethnic groups, but the highest rates are again found amongst Pakistanis and Bangladeshis. One-third of all economically active people of Bangladeshi origin in this age group are unemployed.

Both the Youth Cohort Study (YCS) and the SCPR survey of Scottish ethnic minorities provide further evidence of substantial differences in unemployment rates between different ethnic groups. The YCS also found that whatever definition of unemployment was used, unemployment rates amongst Afro-Caribbeans and South Asians were consistently higher than amongst the white population. The LFS shows the same unemployment rate for ethnic minority men in Scotland as the SCPR survey (19 per cent). This is higher in both surveys than the rate for white men in Scotland, which is 11 per cent according to the LFS and 14 per cent according to the SCPR survey.[3] The LFS shows similar unemployment rates in Scotland for white and ethnic minority women (9 and 8 per cent respectively), but the SCPR study finds an unemployment rate of 21 per cent for ethnic minority women in Scotland, more than double the rate for white women. Within the ethnic minority population, the SCPR study (like the LFS) finds that the highest unemployment rates are among the Pakistanis and the lowest among the Chinese. A number of sources have suggested that unemployment may in fact be a bigger problem among the Chinese population than is apparent from such figures. For example, a report of the Home Affairs Committee about the Chinese community in Britain in the mid-1980s observed that the employment of young people in catering was sometimes no more than a substitute for unemployment. The social stigma surrounding unemployment may discourage some Chinese people from saying that they are without work. The report also said that many families would 'absorb an additional member into the family business even when this was not economically viable, rather than allow him or her to register as unemployed, which is considered shameful'.[4]

Unemployment and job level
Workers in lower job levels are more vulnerable than other workers to unemployment. Table 5.2 shows that the relationship between job level and vulnerability to unemployment is strongest among men. It should be noted that in tables linking rates of unemployment with the characteristics of the last job, these rates are based on respondents who had left their last job within the previous three years. The findings show that the differences in rates of unemployment between ethnic groups are only partly explained by a tendency for ethnic minorities to have been concentrated at lower job levels, which are more vulnerable to unemployment. Within each job level, men from different ethnic groups experience substantially different unemployment rates. Non-manual men are on the whole less likely than manual workers to experience unemployment. White, Indian and Chinese men in the non-manual group have the lowest rate of unemployment (3 per cent), which is similar to that of African Asians and Africans (4 per cent). The rate for non-manual Afro-Caribbeans is about double this, but even within the non-manual group as a whole, men of Pakistani origin have a substantially higher unemployment rate compared with other groups: at 13 per cent, it is over four times the white rate. Looking at the male manual category as a whole, again the white, African Asian and Chinese groups have the lowest unemployment rates (6 or 7 per cent). Afro-Caribbean and Pakistani men in this category have considerably higher rates (11 and 12 per cent respectively), and this time the highest rates of all are found amongst African and Bangladeshi men (18 and 19 per cent respectively). Semi-skilled and unskilled workers have the highest unemployment rates; within this occupational category, there are still substantial differences between ethnic groups.[5] Semi-skilled or unskilled African Asian men have the lowest unemployment rate (5 per cent), half the rate for comparable white men (10 per cent). Indian men in this group have about the same rate (9 per cent) as whites. However, Bangladeshi, Afro-Caribbean and Pakistani men in this category have progressively higher rates of

unemployment; 13, 14 and 16 per cent respectively. Partly or unskilled African men have the highest rate of all (21 per cent).

Thus, controlling for job level explains some but not all of the variation in unemployment rates between ethnic groups. When the comparisons are made within job levels, the difference between whites and ethnic minorities grouped together is reduced, but the differences between specific minority groups become more striking: African Asians and Indians are found to have rates of unemployment similar to those of whites, or lower, whereas Pakistanis and Bangladeshis are found to have much higher rates than whites. Like a number of findings set out in Chapter 4, this suggests that the economic circumstances of specific minority groups are tending to diverge.

Unemployment and region of residence

We found in Chapter 2 that the ethnic minority populations are relatively concentrated in a few geographical areas of the country, in particular the Greater London area, and the Metropolitan Counties in the North and Midlands. Where sample sizes are large enough, we have shown unemployment rates separately for each of the regions having a sizeable ethnic minority population (see Table 5.3). The ideal unit of geographical analysis of unemployment rates would be the 'local labour market', an area of linked local economic activities within which most people both live and work. However, local labour markets cannot be identified separately within the LFS data, which permit only limited regional analysis. More detailed local analysis will have to await the results from the 1991 Census.

Analysis of unemployment rates by region shows that in each region the rate of unemployment among ethnic minorities (taken together) is substantially higher than that among the white population. The pattern in the Greater London area is similar to the national pattern, with African Asian, Indian and Chinese people having slightly higher rates of unemployment than whites. By contrast, Pakistani and Bangladeshi people have substantially higher rates of unemployment, with Afro-Caribbeans somewhere in between.

Outside Greater London, the disparity between ethnic groups is much greater. For example, in Yorkshire and Humberside, the Afro-Caribbean unemployment rate is nearly twice that of whites, and the Pakistani rate is well over double the white rate. In Greater Manchester, the rate for Pakistanis is nearly three times the white rate. In the West Midlands, the disparity between white and ethnic minority unemployment is greatest. In the West Midlands Metropolitan County, all ethnic minority groups have an unemployment rate which is nearly double the white rate, or more than that. Even the groups which nationally have rates nearer to the white population, the African Asians and Indians, have substantially higher rates in this area. In all regions outside London, the ethnic group with the highest rate of unemployment is Pakistanis. In each region, the Pakistani rate is at least double that of whites, and often nearly three times as high. In the region where unemployment among Pakistanis is highest (the West Midlands Metropolitan County), the rate is nearly four times that of white people.

Unemployment and qualifications

Findings presented in Chapter 3 show that there are still some considerable differences in levels of educational and job qualifications between ethnic groups, and these might possibly help to explain the differences in rates of unemployment. Table 5.4 shows, as might be expected, that those with more formal qualifications are less likely to be unemployed. But important differences between ethnic groups still exist within given levels of qualification. For example, among those with A level or equivalent or above, the unemployment rate of 5 per cent among white, African Asian, and Chinese people is less than for other ethnic groups. Pakistanis are again the group with the highest unemployment rate: of Pakistanis qualified to A level or above, 22 per cent are unemployed. Almost a tenth of Pakistanis educated to degree standard are unemployed, compared with 3 per cent of white graduates, and a fifth of Pakistani people with O levels are unemployed, compared to 6 per cent of whites. The sample size is too small to show separate unemployment rates for Bangladeshis with different levels of qualifications. However, the 1986 Home Affairs Committee Report noted the difficulties faced by well-qualified Bangladeshis trying to find work.[6] Of those people with no formal qualifications, the Chinese have the lowest unemployment rate of 8 per cent, compared to a white rate of 12 per cent. Non-qualified African Asians and Indians have higher unemployment rates of 15 and 16 per cent respectively. Over a fifth of non-qualified Afro-Caribbeans, Africans and Pakistanis are unemployed, but it is non-qualified Bangladeshi people who have the highest unemployment rate, at 34 per cent. Thus, level of qualifications does little to explain the differences in unemployment rates between ethnic groups, and striking differences remain when comparisons are made between members of different ethnic groups having similar qualifications.

Drew, Gray and Sime have used the YCS to model the probability of unemployment.[7] They found that attainment level was important in determining the chances of unemployment, in conjunction with gender, social class and ethnic origin.

Unemployment and where the highest qualification was obtained

As set out in Chapter 3, about 36 per cent of ethnic minority people with qualifications gained their highest qualification before coming to Britain. It is important to consider whether unemployment arises partly because foreign qualifications are less highly valued than British ones. If that were the case, then unemployment rates would be higher among those who obtained their highest qualification overseas than among those who obtained a comparable qualification in Britain. Table 5.5 sets out the results of the relevant analysis.

For most ethnic groups, the unemployment rate for those who qualified in the UK is similar that for those who qualified abroad. The exceptions to this pattern are the Africans. Whereas for the whites, those who qualified abroad have slightly higher rates of unemployment than those who are UK-qualified, for Africans with qualifications the reverse is true. African people who qualified outside the UK have substantially *lower* rates of unemployment than those qualified in Britain. Nearly a fifth of UK-qualified African people are unemployed compared with 7 per cent of those who gained their highest qualification outside the UK. However, there is little difference in the case of the other ethnic groups. The overall pattern of unemployment rates which was outlined earlier remains. Whites have lower rates than ethnic minority people, although African Asian and Indian people have low rates relative to other minority populations. The Afro-Caribbeans have higher rates, but the highest unemployment rates are still among the Pakistani population, whether they qualified in the UK or abroad.

Duration of unemployment

Among those unemployed at a particular time, the proportion of people who have been unemployed long-term (for over a year) is roughly similar for the white and ethnic minority populations (Table 5.6). Since the rate of unemployment is higher among the ethnic minorities, this implies, of course, that a higher proportion of the ethnic minority than of the white workforce are long-term unemployed. Of the white unemployed population, 35 per cent have been looking for work for over a year, compared to 39 per cent of the ethnic minority population (taken together). The proportion unemployed for over a year was slightly lower among the African Asian unemployed (31 per cent) than among whites. The Afro-Caribbean and Pakistani unemployed were the most likely to report that they had been out of work for over a year (42 and 48 per cent respectively). In all age groups, male unemployed were more likely than female to have been looking for work for more than a year. The duration of unemployment increases in the older age groups. In the pre-retirement age group, the majority of the unemployed from all ethnic groups have been seeking work for more than a year. Half of the white unemployed in this age group and 59 per cent of the ethnic minority unemployed have spent over a year looking for work. Thus, the higher overall rates of unemployment found among people of Afro-Caribbean and Pakistani origin are associated with a longer than average duration of unemployment, although in this respect the difference between whites and ethnic minorities taken as a whole is not very great.

The YCS results also show that higher rates of unemployment amongst young people of Afro-Caribbean and South Asian origin are associated with a higher incidence of long-term unemployment than amongst whites. The SCPR survey in Scotland actually showed more long-term unemployment amongst the white population than amongst ethnic minorities, although the author stressed that small sample sizes may have made the results unreliable.

Main method of seeking work
Table 5.7 shows the main methods of seeking work reported by unemployed people, by ethnic group. For all persons of working age, the most common method of seeking work is the jobcentre, identified as such by 29 per cent of white, and 28 per cent of ethnic minority unemployed. Unemployed people of Pakistani origin were the most likely of the ethnic groups to report this as the main method. The unemployed from white, Afro-Caribbean and African Asian backgrounds show a similar pattern as regards the main method of seeking work. In all these groups, the three main methods identified (in order of popularity) are jobcentres, studying situations vacant advertisements, and word of mouth. Respectively about a third, a quarter and 7 or 8 per cent of each group reported these as the main method used. A similar proportion of the other racial groups also reported the jobcentre as the most likely method. However, unemployed people of Bangladeshi, Pakistani and Indian origin were more likely than others to report 'word of mouth' as the main method of job search. Of these three groups, 26, 21, and 18 per cent respectively reported word of mouth as their main method of seeking work, compared to 9 per cent of whites. This could be explained by the fact that, in the case of Pakistanis and Bangladeshis at least, the more recently arrived racial minorities are less likely to be familiar with the usual methods of job search and more likely to seek work through people they know and whose language they share. In communities that have relatively low power and influence in the wider society, the importance of intra-community social networks is enhanced. Such networks put people in

touch with the limited range of opportunities available to a disadvantaged minority community.

This idea of informal social networks developing in response to problems of access to public employment services is underlined by the earlier findings on the high level of self-employment among certain minority groups (see Chapter 4). Given the high proportion of self-employed amongst the South Asian community, it is reasonable to argue that in racial groups which have developed their own business networks, word of mouth may well be a more important method of job search than in other communities. The SCPR survey in Scotland also provided some evidence that word of mouth is a relatively more important method of job-search amongst certain ethnic minorities. Of all male ethnic minority householders who were current employees, over half first heard about their job through friends, relatives or acquaintances, compared to 35 per cent of their white counterparts. SCPR found that 67 per cent of the male Chinese employees had heard about their current job in this way, and 47 per cent of South Asians. The jobcentre was a far less popular method of job search (with all groups) than appeared to be the case in the LFS results, with just 7 per cent of white, and 5 per cent of ethnic minority male employees reporting this as the way that they heard about their current job.

Unemployment benefit
Unemployed white people are more likely to be claiming unemployment benefit than people from the ethnic minority groups (Table 5.8). Men are more likely than women to be claiming unemployment benefit.

Of all unemployed white men of working age, 74 per cent reported that they are claiming unemployment benefit, compared to 70 per cent of ethnic minority men (taken together), although the proportion claiming benefit was highest among Pakistani men (80 per cent). There is a similar pattern for unemployed men in each age group, with a slightly higher proportion of the whites reporting that they are claiming benefit than is the case for the ethnic minority men, when taken together (the sample sizes for individual racial minority groups are in most cases too small to analyse them separately within age groups). For women, much lower proportions of the unemployed in all age groups were claiming unemployment benefit: across all ethnic groups, the rate is well below 50 per cent. Among women, there is little difference between ethnic groups in the proportion of the unemployed who were claiming benefit.

The pattern of change

The 1974 and 1982 surveys, and analysis of official statistics, showed that unemployment tended to be higher among Afro-Caribbeans and South Asians than among white people, and that unemployment among ethnic minorities was hyper-cyclical: the minorities were more vulnerable than white people to rising unemployment, but as unemployment fell, they also tended to re-enter the labour market more quickly. Consequently, while there was always a gap in unemployment rates between ethnic minorities and white people, the gap tended to widen substantially at times of high and rising unemployment. Table 5A shows how, even though overall rates of uneployment fell over the decade, there was a continuation of the general pattern of relatively high rates among Afro-Caribbeans, Pakistanis and Bangladeshis. Analysis of the 1984-86 LFS figures (see Table 5.9) shows that during the mid-1980s, when unemployment was reaching its peak before beginning to fall, the gap between the rate for whites and those for certain ethnic minorities was wider than at the end of the decade. For males, the Afro-Caribbean unemployment rate of 26 per cent was more than double that of whites (11 per cent). The rates for Pakistani and Bangladeshi men were almost triple the white rate. Interestingly, the rates for African Asian and Chinese men were almost the same as that for whites, even at a time when the gap between whites and ethnic minorities generally was wider. Figure 5A shows the unemployment rates for whites and ethnic minorities (taken together) for the years between 1984 and 1990.[8] As the general rate of unemployment was falling over the period, the gap between the white and ethnic minority rates became smaller.

Table 5A   Unemployment rates by ethnic group, 1982 and 1988-90

Ethnic group	1982 PSI Survey Men	Women	1988-90 LFS Men	Women
White	13	10	8	7
Afro-Caribbean	25	16	16	13
African Asian	17	21	8	10
Indian	14	18	11	12
Pakistani	29	28	22	25
Bangladeshi	29	*	24	*

*   sample size too small

Figure 5A Unemployment rates, 1984-90

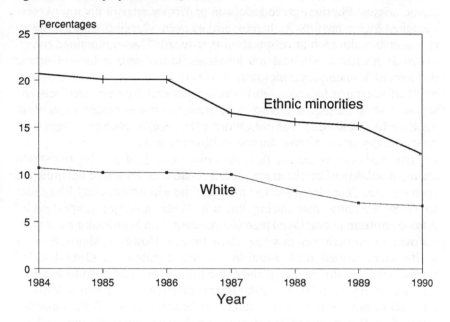

Source: Labour Force Surveys 1984-1990 (GB)

The latest findings on unemployment from the LFS illustrate that while the disparity between whites and ethnic minorities is less, there is still a substantial divergence between specific minority groups. African Asians and Indians now have unemployment rates close to those of white people, whereas the rates among Afro-Caribbeans are still higher, and among Pakistanis and Bangladeshis they remain much higher. These findings cannot be explained in terms of a gradual process of adaptation among groups of immigrant origin. The more recently arrived groups – African Asians and Bangladeshis – are ones with starkly contrasting unemployment rates. Also, the differences between specific ethnic groups are most marked among young people aged 16-24, and in all ethnic groups most of the young will have spent their formative years in Britain. These findings suggest that the differences in vulnerability to unemployment between specific ethnic groups are likely to persist.

The 1982 PSI survey found that differences in job levels were partly responsible for the relatively high rates of unemployment amongst ethnic minorities. The results presented in Chapter 4 showed that those groups with the highest unemployment rates (Afro-Caribbeans, Pakistanis and

Bangladeshis) tend to be found at lower job levels than employees of other ethnic origins. For these three groups in particular rates of unemployment remained higher in 1988-90 than for whites even when job level was taken into account, although the disparity was reduced. Thus it remained true in the mid and late 1980s that job levels explained only a part of ethnic differences in unemployment rates.

In 1982, it was found that differences in unemployment rates between whites and ethnic minorities were not reduced when comparisons were made within regions. In 1988-90, ethnic differences in unemployment rates were actually larger when compared within regions.

The PSI survey found that in 1982, over half of the registered unemployed Afro-Caribbean and South Asian men had been unemployed for over a year, compared to about a third of the white men. The LFS figures for 1984-86 show that during the mid-1980s a larger proportion of Afro-Caribbean unemployed men (62 per cent) had been looking for work for over a year than men of other ethnic groups. However, almost half the white unemployed men were in the same category. Over half of unemployed Indian, Pakistani and Bangladeshi men had been looking for over a year. By 1988-90, the differences between ethnic groups in terms of unemployment duration were smaller, although it was still the case that more of the Pakistani and Afro-Caribbean men had been seeking work for more than a year.

The LFS agrees with other sources in showing that people of Pakistani and Bangladeshi origin rely more on word of mouth (probably within their own ethnic communities) as a method of job search than do members of other ethnic groups. We do not have information from 1982 about methods of seeking work. Table 5.10 shows the main methods used by unemployed people according to the 1984-86 LFS figures. We can see that during the mid-1980s, the jobcentre was a more popular method of looking for work amongst people of all ethnic groups than was the case at the end of the decade. This may be related to the reduction of job search services that jobcentres provide for non-claimants, and to the integration of jobcentres with unemployment benefit offices, both of which occurred after the mid-1980s. Studying the situations vacant became slightly more popular amongst unemployed people of all ethnic groups over the 1980s. Word of mouth was a more common method of seeking work for Indian, Pakistani and Bangladeshi people in 1984-86, as was the case at the end of the decade.

The analysis set out in this chapter has tested one by one a number of factors that might help to explain the gap in unemployment rates: age, job level, region, level of qualifications. The contrast in unemployment rates is reduced when comparisons are made within job levels, but it remains very marked. The other factors do little to explain differences in rates of unemployment between ethnic groups, and in some respects the contrast is enhanced when these factors are taken into account. For example, differences in rates of unemployment between ethnic groups are particularly marked within the West Midlands region, and among young people.

Notes
1. The argument was originally put in D.J. Smith, *The Facts of Racial Disadvantage*, PEP, 1976. The term 'hyper-cyclical' was first used in this context in S. Field et al., *Ethnic Minorities in Britain*, Home Office Research Study Np.68, HMSO, 1981.
2. See, for example, D.J. Smith, *Unemployment and Racial Minority Groups*, PSI, 1980; 'Ethnic Origins and the Labour Market', *Employment Gazette*, March 1990, February 1991 and February 1993.
3. The sample for the SCPR study was not nationally representative. The higher SCPR figure for white male uneployment in Scotland is probably explained by the fact that the white sample was drawn from the same areas as the ethnic minority sample.
4. House of Commons, Second Report from the Home Affairs Committee, Session 1984-5, *Chinese Community in Britain*, para 108.
5. Note that the semi-skilled and unskilled category is included within the total manual category previously considered.
6. House of Commons, Home Affairs Committee, First Report Session 1986-87, *Bangadeshis in Britain*.
7. David Drew, John Gray and Nicholas Sime, *Against the Odds: the Education and Labour Market Experiences of Black Young People*, Youth Cohort Study: England and Wales: Department of Employment, 1992.
8. The Figure shows the combined rate for all ethnic minorities because sample sizes for the different ethnic minority groups in single years would be too small.

Table 5.1 Unemployment rates by ethnic group, age and sex, 1988-90

Percentages

	Age 16-59/64			Age 16-24			Age 25-44			Age 45-59/64		
	All	M	F	All	M	F	All	M	F	All	M	F
All origins	8	8	7	11	12	10	7	6	7	7	7	5
White	7	8	7	10	11	9	7	6	7	6	7	5
Total ethnic minority	13	14	12	19	20	19	11	11	11	12	13	10
Afro-Caribbean	14	16	13	23	24	23	12	11	12	11	15	6
African Asian	9	8	10	12	9	15	7	6	8	13	11	17
Indian	11	11	12	16	18	13	10	9	11	11	11	13
Pakistani	22	22	25	30	31	30	18	18	18	22	21	*
Bangladeshi	24	24	*	19	15	*	23	26	*	33	33	*
Chinese	7	9	4	7	*	*	9	12	4	2	2	*
African	14	15	13	27	28	26	10	13	7	11	7	*
Other/Mixed	10	9	12	13	14	11	10	8	14	6	5	7

Source: 1988, 1989, 1990 Labour Force Surveys (GB)

* Sample size too small

Percentages

Table 5.2   Unemployment rates within job levels by ethnic group, 1988-90

	Non-manual			All Manual			Partly or Unskilled Manual		
	All	M	F	All	M	F	All	M	F
All origins	3	3	4	7	7	6	8	10	6
White	3	3	4	7	7	6	8	10	6
Total ethnic minority	5	5	6	10	10	9	10	12	8
Afro-Caribbean	7	8	7	10	11	8	10	14	6
African Asian	4	4	5	7	6	8	7	5	8
Indian	4	3	5	9	9	9	9	9	9
Pakistani	13	13	13	12	12	10	15	16	13
Bangladeshi	9	7	*	19	19	*	12	13	*
Chinese	3	3	3	6	6	4	7	*	*
African	4	4	4	13	18	7	13	21	6
Other/Mixed	4	4	4	10	7	15	11	10	13

Source: 1988, 1989, 1990 Labour Force Surveys (GB)

* Sample size too small

125

Table 5.3 Regional rates of unemployment, by ethnic group, 1988-90

	All origins	White	Total ethnic minority	Afro-Caribbeans	African Asian	Indian	Pakistani	Bangla-deshi	Chinese	African	Other/Mixed
Region											
South East Region	6	5	11	13	7	10	17	22	7	13	10
Greater London	7	7	13	14	7	11	21	23	9	14	13
Yorkshire and Humberside Region	9	9	16	17	8	15	22	*	*	*	8
North West Region	10	10	18	14	*	13	26	*	*	*	15
Greater Manchester	10	10	20	18	*	13	27	*	*	*	13
West Midlands Region	8	7	17	19	14	14	29	*	*	*	17
West Midlands Metropolitan County	9	8	18	19	15	15	31	*	*	*	*
East Midlands Region	7	7	13	15	10	14	*	*	*	*	*

Source: 1988, 1989, 1990 Labour Force Surveys (GB)

* Sample size too small

Table 5.4   Unemployment rate and highest qualification by ethnic group, 1988-90

Percentages

Highest qualification	All quali- fications	Higher (A-Level+)	Degree/ equivalent	O-Level equivalent	None
All origins	8	5	3	7	12
White	7	5	3	6	12
Total ethnic minority	13	9	6	13	18
Afro-Caribbean	14	9	2	14	20
African Asian	9	5	3	9	15
Indian	11	8	3	12	16
Pakistani	22	22	9	21	24
Bangladeshi	24	*	*	*	34
Chinese	7	5	5	4	8
African	14	11	8	15	22
Other/Mixed	10	9	10	12	10

Source: 1988, 1989, 1990 Labour Force Surveys (GB)

*   Sample size too small

Table 5.5   Unemployment rates of those with highest qualification gained in UK and abroad, by ethnic group, 1988-90

Percentages

Where gained qualification	Qualification gained in UK			Qualification gained abroad			All qualifications		
	All	M	F	All	M	F	All	M	F
Ethnic group (all with qualifications)									
All origins	6	6	6	8	7	9	6	6	6
White	6	5	6	7	6	8	6	5	6
Total ethnic minority	11	11	12	10	9	10	11	10	11
Afro-Caribbean	13	12	14	10	11	8	12	12	13
African Asian	7	5	10	7	7	6	7	6	8
Indian	10	10	9	9	8	11	9	9	10
Pakistani	21	20	24	19	16	*	20	18	26
Bangladeshi	10	*	*	*	*	*	11	12	*
Chinese	5	6	2	7	9	6	6	7	4
African	19	19	18	7	8	6	13	14	12
Other/Mixed	9	8	10	11	8	15	10	8	12

Source: 1988, 1989, 1990 Labour Force Surveys (GB)

*Sample size too small

Table 5.6 Percentage of unemployed seeking work for over a year, by ethnic group, 1988-90

Percentages

All unemployed of working age	Age 16-59/64			Age 16-24			Age 25-44			Age 45-59/64		
	All	M	F	All	M	F	All	M	F	All	M	F
All origins	36	45	23	24	28	18	36	49	20	50	56	13
White	35	45	22	23	28	17	36	50	19	50	55	38
Total ethnic minority	39	45	29	30	31	28	36	43	27	59	66	41
Afro-Caribbean	42	51	29	33	42	22	39	*	32	61	66	*
African Asian	31	*	*	*	*	*	24	*	*	*	*	*
Indian	39	46	30	25	*	*	38	49	*	55	*	*
Pakistani	48	50	41	33	*	*	48	53	*	*	*	*
Bangladeshi	32	*	*	*	*	*	*	*	*	*	*	*
Chinese	*	*	*	*	*	*	*	*	*	*	*	*
African	37	*	*	*	*	*	*	*	*	*	*	*
Other/Mixed	28	*	26	*	*	*	24	*	*	*	*	*

Source: 1988, 1989, 1990 Labour force Surveys (GB)

* Sample size too small

Table 5.7 Main method of seeking work in last 4 weeks, all unemployed of working age, by ethnic group, 1988-90

Column Percentages

Main method used	All origins	White	Total ethnic minority	Afro-Caribbeans	African Asian	Indian	Pakistani	Bangla-deshi	Chinese	African	Other/Mixed
Job centre	29	29	28	30	32	26	34	22	*	26	20
Private agency	2	2	2	2	1	2	1	0	*	3	3
Advertise in the press	0	0	0	0	0	1	0	0	*	3	1
Answer press ads	10	10	10	14	9	6	5	5	*	22	12
Study sits vac	26	27	21	23	25	19	18	14	*	21	22
Apply direct to firm	8	8	8	7	8	8	7	18	*	4	10
Word of mouth	9	9	14	8	7	18	21	26	*	4	16
Waiting result	2	2	1	1	1	2	2	0	*	2	0
Anything else	4	4	4	3	4	5	1	4	*	3	4
Not seeking work in last 4 weeks	8	8	9	9	10	9	6	8	*	10	10
No answer	2	2	3	2	2	5	4	3	*	2	1

Source: 1988, 1989, 1990 Labour Force Surveys (GB)

*Sample size too small

Table 5.8 Percentage of unemployed claiming unemployment benefit, by ethnic group, 1988-90

Percentages

	Age 16-59/64			Age 16-24			Age 25-44			Age 45-59/64		
	All	M	F	All	M	F	All	M	F	All	M	F
All origins	60	73	40	61	70	49	59	80	33	59	68	42
White	60	74	40	62	70	49	59	81	32	59	68	42
Total ethnic Minority	58	70	39	55	65	42	60	77	34	59	65	44
Afro-Caribbean	58	70	42	60	75	42	59	*	42	53	56	*
African Asian	58	*	*	*	*	*	65	*	*	*	*	*
Indian	55	65	39	50	*	*	56	80	*	59	*	*
Pakistani	73	80	49	74	*	*	73	83	*	*	*	*
Bangladeshi	69	*	*	*	*	*	*	*	*	*	*	*
Chinese	*	*	*	*	*	*	*	*	*	*	*	*
African	41	*	*	*	*	*	*	*	*	*	*	*
Other/Mixed	49	58	39	*	*	*	47	*	*	*	*	*

Source: 1988, 1989, 1990 Labour Force Surveys (GB)

* Sample size too small

131

Table 5.9 Unemployment rates by ethnic group, age and sex, 1984-86

Percentages

	Age 16-59/64			Age 16-24			Age 25-44			Age 45-59/64		
	All	M	F	All	M	F	All	M	F	All	M	F
All origins	11	11	10	18	19	16	10	10	10	8	8	6
White	11	11	10	17	18	15	9	9	10	7	8	6
Total ethnic minority	20	21	19	32	32	31	16	17	15	17	19	12
Afro-Caribbean	22	26	19	34	37	30	17	21	14	16	19	12
African Asian	13	12	15	21	21	22	11	10	12	11	11	*
Indian	18	18	19	29	27	33	16	17	16	14	15	11
Pakistani	31	30	40	47	44	*	25	25	27	32	30	*
Bangladeshi	32	31	*	*	*	*	26	26	*	42	43	*
Chinese	11	12	9	*	*	*	26	25	29	15	16	*
African	26	25	28	39	*	*	26	25	29	15	16	*
Other/Mixed	17	15	20	31	29	34	12	11	15	11	12	9

* Sample size too small

Source: 1984, 1985, 1986 Labour Force Surveys (GB)

Table 5.10 Main method of seeking work in last 4 weeks, all unemployed of working age, by ethnic group, 1984-86

Column Percentages

	All origins	White	Total ethnic minority	Afro-Caribbean	African Asian	Indian	Pakistani	Bangla-deshi	Chinese	African	Other/Mixed
Job centre	38	37	40	43	45	40	40	37	23	40	33
Private agency	1	1	2	3	2	1	0	0	*	2	1
Advertise in press	0	0	0	0	0	0	0	0	*	0	0
Answer press ads.	12	12	10	12	11	10	7	4	*	19	9
Study sits. vac.	22	22	15	17	11	15	13	3	*	17	24
Apply direct to firm	8	8	10	9	13	8	9	21	*	8	8
Word of mouth	9	9	14	8	11	17	21	24	*	9	16
Waiting result	1	2	1	1	1	3	0	0	*	1	1
Anything else	1	1	1	0	1	0	0	0	*	0	1
Not seeking work in last 4 weeks	5	5	4	4	2	2	5	7	*	2	5
No answer	2	2	3	2	1	5	3	4	*	2	3

Source: 1984, 1985, 1986 Labour Force Surveys (GB)

* Sample size too small

6 Housing

The 1974 and 1982 surveys documented the development of tenure patterns amongst Afro-Caribbean and South Asian people up until the early 1980s. They described the tendency of newly-arrived immigrants to find housing in the most accessible part of the UK housing market, the private rented sector. Once they were joined by their dependents and family units were established, they needed to find larger and more secure accommodation. Because of qualifying periods of residency needed to obtain council housing, the only option to many immigrants was to buy what were often the cheaper properties on the market. In this way, dramatic differences in both the tenure patterns and the quality of housing developed between the South Asian population, the Afro-Caribbean population and the white population. In particular, amongst whites the more affluent people tended to be owner occupiers of better standard housing, whereas amongst ethnic minorities the situation was very different. Despite being relatively recent arrivals, and often being in the poorer jobs, both Afro-Caribbean and South Asian populations achieved over a short time the same, and higher, degrees of owner occupation as the indigenous population. Whereas among the general population, the level of owner occupation increases with rising affluence, and is therefore greater among those at higher as compared with lower job levels, among South Asians, owner occupation was, paradoxically, most common amongst the lower job levels.

In 1974, a very low level of council house occupation was another notable feature of the tenure pattern of South Asians, relative both to whites and to Afro-Caribbeans. There were two factors that might help to explain this pattern. South Asians were the more recently-arrived immigrant groups, so were more likely to be excluded from council housing by residence qualifications; and having poor English many recently arrived South Asians preferred to live close to members of their own group. In 1974, the Afro-Caribbean population had about the same level of owner occupation as whites overall, but as in the case of South Asians, the proportion who were owner occupiers increased among those at the lower job levels. Also, within each job level, the proportion of Afro-Caribbeans in owner occupation was higher than for whites at that job level. Already by 1974 there was a higher level of council house occupation among Afro-Caribbeans than among South Asians, and by 1982 council house tenancies among Afro-Caribbeans had risen to about the same level as among the white population. For both main groups, the paradoxically high level of owner occupation among those at lower job levels could partly be seen as a response to the closure of other housing opportunities, particularly at the early stages of settlement. However, the remarkable pattern of findings also seemed to imply a positive drive towards home ownership associated with the drive towards self improvement and capital accumulation that is typical of immigrant communities.

This chapter examines the pattern of tenure which existed amongst the various racial groups at the end of the 1980s. This decade saw a number of major developments in the UK housing market; in particular, the increasing proportion of council tenants who exercised the 'right to buy' their homes under the 1980 Housing Act and the Tenants' Rights (Scotland) Act 1980. These Acts gave tenants of local authorities (as well as those of some other public bodies) the right to buy their homes if they had been tenants with security of tenure for at least 3 years (this qualifying period was reduced to 2 years in 1984). It is important to consider whether such developments have caused any changes in the pattern of tenure for different racial groups. The chapter will analyse overall patterns of tenure and the relationship with social class and household type. The LFS does not include questions on dwelling type or housing quality, although we include some such details from the General Household Survey (GHS) report of 1989.

Tenure patterns
Table 6.1 shows the tenure patterns for all households in Great Britain according to ethnic group of the head of household. In broad terms, the patterns are consistent with the findings of earlier research. For example, there are still very high (both relative and absolute) levels of owner occupation amongst the South Asian groups, with the exception of the Bangladeshis. Over three-quarters of African Asian, Indian and Pakistani households are owner occupied, compared to 65 per cent of white households. About the same proportion of Afro-Caribbean and Bangladeshi households are owner occupied (45 and 46 per cent), and African households are least likely to be owner occupied, with only 31 per cent in this category. The private rented sector is comparatively more important for the ethnic groups with higher proportions of recently-arrived people, the Bangladeshis and the Africans (10 and 17 per cent of all households respectively, compared to 7 per cent of white households). However, the group with the highest proportion of households in the private rented sector

is the Chinese (21 per cent). The public housing sector still accounts for a quarter of all white households, but 43 and 41 per cent of African and Afro-Caribbean households rent from a local authority. Housing associations are more important in the Afro-Caribbean population than in any other, though they account for only a small proportion of total households (6 per cent compared to 2 per cent of white households).

These figures are comparable to those produced in the 1989 GHS report, which covers the years 1987-89. The GHS reported that 64 per cent of households headed by a white person are owner-occupied, compared to 74 per cent of those headed by an Indian, 67 per cent of those headed by a Pakistani or Bangladeshi, and 47 per cent of those headed by an Afro-Caribbean person. The GHS figures for council tenancies also compare closely with the LFS. The GHS shows 25 per cent of white households in council tenancies, and 8 per cent of Indian, 17 per cent of Pakistani/Bangladeshi and 42 per cent of Afro-Caribbean households in this category. The SCPR survey in Scotland (which covered South Asian and Chinese people) also found a very high incidence of owner-occupation in the South Asian population. The rates were about 80 per cent compared to 51 per cent of the white population.

Tenure and job level
Owner occupation and job level
Table 6.2 shows the high incidence of owner occupation in the population as a whole in the late 1980s, amongst people of all job levels. Amongst the white population, owner occupation peaks at 88 per cent of those in the top category (households of professionals, managers and employers).[1] As job level (of head of household) decreases, so does the proportion of owner occupation, but to a lesser degree than has been found before. For example, three quarters of skilled manual white households are owner occupied, and even among the families of unskilled workers 44 per cent of households are owner occupied. In the South Asian population, we still see a high degree of owner occupation in the lower job levels compared to the white population. For example, for each of the three main south Asian groups (African Asians, Indians and Pakistanis) over 80 per cent of households in the manual category are owner occupied compared with 69 per cent of white households headed by a manual worker. For Afro-Caribbean households however, the inverse relationship between job level and incidence of owner occupation seems to have disappeared; 69 per cent of professional, managerial and employer households are owner occupied, and a similar proportion of skilled manual households, but this falls to 51 per cent in semi-skilled households, and 35 per cent of unskilled manual households.

For the other ethnic groups, sample sizes permit only a comparison of all non-manual with all manual. This shows lower levels of owner occupation in general, and again higher levels among non-manual than among manual households; this disparity is greater than for other ethnic groups.

Amongst unemployed people (not shown in the table), there is a similar pattern of owner occupation between different ethnic groups to the overall pattern outlined above. Indian and Pakistani households still show a high incidence of owner occupation (63 and 75 per cent), Afro-Caribbeans have a relatively low incidence, with white households in between. For households containing retired people (not shown), a similar incidence of owner occupation is apparent for white and ethnic minority households, although it is slightly higher among whites.

Local authority housing and job level
Table 6.3 shows the incidence of council housing as a form of tenure amongst households from the different ethnic groups. Once again, the previously-noted relationship with job level still holds in the white population, though the absolute proportions of households which are rented from the local authority are smaller than in the past. Within the top job level (professional, managerial, employer), the proportion of white households in council housing is very small (3 per cent), but this rises to 17 per cent in the skilled manual and 44 per cent in the unskilled categories. The low incidence of council tenancy amongst the South Asian population remains apparent, in comparison with all other groups: the proportion of households in council accommodation in the African Asian, Indian and Pakistani populations is below 10 per cent in both non-manual and manual categories in all these groups. Bangladeshi households stand out from the other South Asian groups in that they have a relatively high incidence of council tenancy in both non-manual and manual categories (17 and 33 per cent respectively). Afro-Caribbeans and Africans are also groups with relatively high degrees of council tenancy. Among non-manual households, 29 per cent of Afro-Caribbeans and 26 per cent of Africans are in council accommodation. This rises to 30 and 43 per cent respectively in the manual category. (This marks another change from previous studies; even by 1982, within job levels the proportion of Afro-Caribbeans in council housing was much lower than was the case for the general population. This pattern has now reversed.)

Amongst the households of unemployed people (not shown in tables), the proportion of households in council housing within each ethnic group is, not surprisingly, higher than for the working population. However, a similar overall pattern applies, with lower incidence of council tenancy amongst the South Asian populations than amongst whites, and a higher proportion of Afro-Caribbean and African householders being council tenants. Among the households of retired people (not shown in tables), a slightly lower proportion of white than of ethnic minority households are in council tenancies (28 compared with 34 per cent).

Household type and tenure

Another possible explanation of variations in tenure patterns is the different mix of household types in the different ethnic groups. Table 6.4 shows the owner occupation patterns for the different ethnic groups according to household type. In some cells the sample sizes are too small to permit detailed comparisons, but it is clear that the overall pattern of owner occupation remains. Within each type of household,[2] the South Asians (bar the Bangladeshis) have high incidence of owner occupation compared to whites, while Afro-Caribbean and African households have a lower incidence. The highest incidence of owner occupation is found in South Asian households in the 'large family' category in which 88, 89 and 83 per cent of African Asian, Indian and Pakistani households respectively are owner occupied.

Table 6.5 shows the proportion of households from each ethnic group which rent accommodation from the local authority; and again the general pattern outlined above remains. However, the disparity between South Asian, white and Afro-Caribbean households is greatest within the 'large family' type, which forms a major proportion of all South Asian households. Nevertheless, the general pattern remains across all household types: that is, a higher proportion of Afro-Caribbean and African households than of white households are in council tenancies, and a lower proportion of South Asian households. Also, for each household type, it remains true that a higher proportion of Afro-Caribbean households than of households belonging to other ethnic groups are renting from a housing association.

Type of accommodation and density of occupation[3]

The LFS does not provide information on the type of accommodation (flat, terraced house, etc.) or density of occupation, for example in relation to the 'bedroom standard'. However, some information on these topics can be drawn from the GHS. These findings are based on a much smaller sample than the LFS, but it is encouraging that the tenure patterns of ethnic minorities shown by the two surveys are similar.

Households headed by a white person are more often than ethnic minority households found in detached or semi-detached houses, the respective proportions being 52 and 28 per cent. South Asians have a relatively large proportion of households living in terraced housing when compared with other groups: about 50 per cent of South Asian households are in terraced housing compared with 29 per cent of white households, and 37 per cent of Afro-Caribbean households. Afro-Caribbean households have a larger proportion than other groups living in flats or maisonettes (29 per cent of Afro-Caribbean households, compared with 14 per cent of white, 12 per cent of Pakistani or Bangladeshi, and 6 per cent of Indian households).

The GHS provides two indicators of density of occupation: number of bedrooms in relation to the bedroom standard, and number of persons per room. These suggested that in general, white households have more space than ethnic minority households. Whilst about 6 per cent of white households have over one person per room, this compares with 12 per cent of Afro-Caribbean, 22 per cent of Indian, and 43 per cent of Pakistani or Bangladeshi households. The GHS found only 2 per cent of white households with one or more bedrooms below the standard, compared to 10 per cent of Afro-Caribbean, 13 per cent of Indian, and 28 per cent of Pakistani or Bangladeshi households.

The Scottish survey carried out by SPCR also included some information on accommodation type. This showed that in Scotland slightly fewer ethnic minority households than white ones are living in houses, and slightly more living in flats, maisonettes or bedsits. Like the GHS, SCPR found that the density of occupation in ethnic minority households is greater than in white households. Pakistani households are particularly likely to be found in densely occupied accommodation, with 29 per cent in accommodation with more than 1.5 persons per room.

The pattern of change

The surveys of 1974 and 1982 showed a highly unusual pattern of tenure among Afro-Caribbeans and South Asians. There was a high level of owner occupation among South Asians, and a paradoxical tendency for owner occupation to be greater among those at lower than at higher job levels. Among Afro-Caribbeans, there was a similar level of owner occupation to that found among the white population. At the early stages of the migration, very few of the migrants from any group managed to penetrate into council housing. By 1982, however, the proportion of Afro-Caribbeans in council housing was higher overall than the proportion of whites, although the opposite was true when comparisons were made within job levels. The proportion of South Asians in council housing remained much lower than for whites.

The LFS findings for 1988-90 show some important changes from the 1982 pattern. Among the general population, owner occupation has grown, and has spread to the lower socio-economic levels: consequently, the level of owner occupation is now much less strongly related to socio-economic group than it was ten years ago. At the same time, the paradoxical relationship between socio-economic group and owner occupation among ethnic minorities has disappeared, so that the pattern among ethnic minorities and that among white people are now much more similar. Nevertheless, the level of owner occupation among South Asians, with the exception of Bangladeshis, remains very high. These findings are consistent with the view that whereas some South Asians were in the past forced into owner occupation because of the lack of any alternative, owner occupation is now the housing of choice for most South Asians. The Bangladeshis are an interesting exception. Their low level of owner occupation is consistent with their low socio-economic status, and their recent arrival in Britain; but whereas previous waves of South Asian migrants were initially excluded from council housing, a substantial proportion of Bangladeshis are now housed in the public sector.

The development of the situation outlined in this chapter can clearly be seen in Table 6A below, which shows the rates of owner-occupation for households of different ethnic groups in 1982, 1984-86 (taken from Table 6.6) and 1988-90.

Table 6A Percentage of households owner-occupied by ethnic group during the 1980s[1]

Ethnic group	1982 PSI Survey	1984-86 LFS	1988-90 LFS
White	59	60	65
Afro-Caribbean	41	38	46
African Asian	73	81	82
Indian	77	77	76
Pakistani	80	78	75
Bangladeshi	30	31	46

[1] It should be noted that the definition of households used in the 1982 survey differs somewhat from that used in the analysis of the LFS data. The 1982 survey defined an Afro-Caribbean household as a household containing any adult who was Afro-Caribbean, and so on for other minority ethnic groups. In our analysis of the LFS, an Afro-Caribbean household is defined as any household headed by an Afro-Caribbean person.

This table shows that in terms of overall tenure patterns, the main change over the 1980s has been a steady growth in home ownership amongst the white and Bangladeshi populations in particular, but also in the Afro-Caribbean population. The growth in owner occupation in the Bangladeshi population in the last few years is quite striking. As recently as 1986 the Home Affairs Committee reported that a smaller proportion of Bangladeshi dwellings are owner-occupied than is the case among any other ethnic minority.[4] Owner-occupation amongst those populations in which it has traditionally been high (African Asians, Indians and Pakistanis) has remained fairly stable. The fact that the main change has occurred in the lower socio-economic groups is illustrated by the fact that in 1982, the level of owner-occupation amongst white households of which the head was an unskilled manual worker was just 21 per cent. By the mid-1980s (according to the LFS), this had risen to 39 per cent, and by the end of the decade was 44 per cent. This may reflect the fact that levels of owner occupation among white people in the top socio-economic group have been high for some time. Any increase would have to be at the lower socio-economic levels.

Table 6B   **Percentage of households renting from local authority by ethnic group during the 1980s**

Ethnic group	1982 PSI Survey	1984-86 LFS	1988-90 LFS
White	30	28	25
Afro-Caribbean	46	47	41
African Asian	19	8	9
Indian	16	12	11
Pakistani	13	13	11
Bangladeshi	53	49	36

Table 6B shows a steady fall over the 1980s in the proportion of white households who were in council tenancies. In fact households from all ethnic minority populations became gradually less likely to be in this category, but the Afro-Caribbeans and Bangladeshis were moving from relatively high proportions of council tenancies, and remained at the end of the decade more likely than other ethnic groups to be in this kind of housing. In the other South Asian groups, the proportion of households renting from local authorities fell from what were already relatively low levels.

The 1982 survey did include details about dwelling type and number of persons per room. Then it was found that 54 per cent of white households were living in semi-detached or detached houses, compared to 23 per cent of Afro-Caribbean and 26 per cent of South Asian households. According to the latest GHS figures, this position has not changed a great deal over the 1980s. Similarly, the high proportion of South Asian households living in terraced housing has continued over the 1980s. In 1982, PSI found that 59 per cent of South Asian households were living in terraced housing. This figure is still about 50 per cent at the end of the 1980s.

The 1982 survey found that about 3 per cent of white households had more than one person per room, compared with 16 per cent of Afro-Caribbean, 26 per cent of Indian, 47 per cent of Pakistani and 60 per cent of Bangladeshi households. The GHS figures quoted earlier suggest that the differences between white and ethnic minority households on this measure have narrowed slightly over the last decade, but that the general pattern which existed in 1982 still remains. A more detailed set of comparisons of housing quality would require analysis at the local level, since a large proportion of the ethnic minority population in Britain is found in the conurbations, where the lower quality accommodation tends to be located. Comparison at the national level will inevitably find much greater differences between white and ethnic minority accommodation than would be found by local level analysis, since the ethnic minority population has traditionally been concentrated into inner-city areas associated with lower quality housing.

Notes
1. Households are classified according to the socio-economic group of the head.
2. For definition of household type, see notes to Table 2.9.
3. The information in this section is drawn from the General Household Survey. See E. Breeze, G. Trevor and A. Wilmot, *General Household Survey 1989*, OPCS Survey Division, London: HMSO (1991), Table 2.54.
4. House of Commons, First report from the Home Affairs Committee, Session 1986-87, *Bangladeshis in Britain*, para.20.

Table 6.1   Tenure patterns by ethnic group (all households), 1988-90

Column Percentages

	All origins	White	Total ethnic minority	Afro-Caribbean	African Asian	Indian	Pakistani	Bangla-deshi	Chinese	African	Other/Mixed
Owner-occupied	64	65	59	45	83	77	76	45	52	31	52
Rented from Local Authority	25	25	24	41	9	11	11	36	19	43	23
Rented from Housing Assn	2	2	3	6	1	1	1	2	4	4	4
Rented-Other	8	7	11	6	5	9	10	9	21	17	19
Other	1	1	2	2	1	2	2	7	4	4	1

Source: 1988, 1989, 1990 Labour Force Surveys (GB)

143

**Table 6.2 Owner occupation among households by ethnic group and job level
of head of household, 1988-90**

Percentage of households owner-occupiers

Job level of head of household	All Non-manual	Professional/ Manager/ Employer	Other Non-manual	All Manual	Skilled Manual	Semi-skilled Manual	Unskilled Manual
All origins	85	88	79	69	75	57	44
White	85	88	80	69	75	57	44
Total ethnic minority	71	76	65	69	76	62	51
Afro-Caribbean	57	69	51	58	67	51	35
African Asian	87	86	89	85	87	*	*
Indian	84	85	82	86	87	84	*
Pakistani	81	79	*	81	85	76	*
Bangladeshi	*	*	*	*	*	*	*
Chinese	65	66	*	59	*	*	*
African	54	66	47	35	40	.*	*
Other/Mixed	66	65	67	59	70	45	*

Source: 1988, 1989, 1990 Labour Force Surveys (GB)

*   Sample size too small

**Table 6.3 Local authority housing by ethnic group and job level of head of
household, 1988-90**

Percentage of households in council tenancies

Job level of head of household	All Non-manual	Professional/ Manager/ Employer	Other Non-manual	All Manual	Skilled Manual	Semi-skilled Manual	Unskilled Manual
All origins	6	3	10	22	17	29	44
White	6	3	9	22	17	29	44
Total ethnic minority	13	7	20	19	15	24	33
Afro-Caribbean	29	19	34	30	23	37	46
African Asian	6	5	6	9	6	*	*
Indian	3	2	6	7	7	6	*
Pakistani	6	5	*	9	6	12	*
Bangladeshi	*	*	*	33	*	*	*
Chinese	6	5	*	24	*	*	*
African	26	17	32	43	39	*	*
Other/Mixed	11	9	13	25	18	38	*

Source: 1988, 1989, 1990 Labour Force Surveys (GB)

*   Sample size too small

Table 6.4   Rates of owner occupation and ethnic group by household type, 1988-90

Percentage households in owner-occupied

Household type	1 adult 16-59	2 adults 16-59	Small family	Large family	Adult household	1 or 2 60+[1]
All origins	54	77	69	63	74	64
White	55	77	69	62	74	64
Total ethnic minority	35	63	56	70	72	59
Afro-Caribbean	30	60	41	32	68	51
African Asian	*	*	79	88	81	*
Indian	43	74	79	89	82	64
Pakistani	*	63	59	83	84	*
Bangladeshi	*	*	*	48	*	*
Chinese	*	64	65	36	55	*
African	19	39	33	31	42	*
Other/Mixed	39	61	47	52	65	*

Source: 1988, 1989, 1990 Labour Force Surveys (GB)

*   Sample size too small

1   For definitions see footnotes to Table 2.9.

Table 6.5   Local authority housing and ethnic group by household type, 1988-90

Percentage of households in council tenancies

Household type	1 adult 16-59	2 adults 16-59	Small family	Large family	Adult household	1 or 2 60+
All origins	24	12	23	30	18	28
White	23	12	23	32	18	28
Total ethnic minority	33	15	29	21	16	28
Afro-Caribbean	47	25	47	58	24	36
African Asian	*	*	12	7	12	*
Indian	23	8	10	6	10	22
Pakistani	*	15	17	9	6	*
Bangladeshi	*	*	*	38	*	*
Chinese	*	4	18	45	11	*
African	42	32	52	48	31	*
Other/Mixed	18	9	30	32	16	*

Source: 1988, 1989, 1990 Labour Force Surveys (GB)

*   Sample size too small

Table 6.6 Tenure patterns by ethnic group (all households), 1984-86

Column Percentages

	All origins	White	Total ethnic minority	Afro-Caribbean	African Asian	Indian	Pakistani	Bangla-deshi	Chinese	African	Other/Mixed
Owner-occupied	60	60	55	38	81	77	78	31	48	31	43
Rented from local authority	28	28	28	47	8	12	13	49	24	39	25
Rented from housing association	2	2	4	7	1	2	1	5	3	6	4
Rented - other	9	9	12	7	9	8	8	14	24	23	27
Other	1	1	1	1	1	1	1	2	1	1	0

Source: 1984, 1985, 1986 Labour Force Surveys (GB)

7 Conclusions

A striking feature of the previous studies on the circumstances of Britain's ethnic minority population has been the continuity of the patterns which developed after the first wave of immigration in the 1950s. Arriving in a new country, migrants experienced a number of constraints on their life chances which were to continue to exert an influence decades later. Some of the difficulties stemmed from the need to adapt to an unfamiliar language and culture, and would be experienced by most migrant populations. By far the most important constraint was their experience of widespread discrimination, both direct and indirect, in many aspects of their lives. Research in the 1960s showed that such discrimination was the major factor behind racial disadvantage in Britain.

Immigrant communities found themselves restricted to a particular niche of the labour market. They tended to be found in particular industries and types of job within those industries. In general, ethnic minority workers were in low-status and poorly-paid jobs compared to whites. Whilst it was true that, on the whole, ethnic minority people were less likely than whites to hold formal qualifications, research showed that even among those with a given level of qualifications, ethnic minority people were still in much poorer jobs than whites. As chronic unemployment began to be a permanent feature of the British economy from the early 1970s on, ethnic minority people continuously suffered from higher rates of unemployment than their white counterparts. Again, this was partly attributable to the over-representation of ethnic minority people in those jobs which were more vulnerable to unemployment. But even within job levels, unemployment was persistently higher than for whites.

In the housing market, people from different minority ethnic groups developed sharply contrasting patterns of tenure, both from each other and from the white population. South Asian people very quickly reached levels of owner-occupation which were greater than or equal to those of the white population. Owner-occupation was actually higher among the lower socio-economic groups; the reverse situation to that in the white population, where owner-occupation was associated with affluence. This was because, for South Asian people, owner-occupation was a way of obtaining poor quality housing at low cost. Levels of owner-occupation were much lower among people of Afro-Caribbean origin. Research in the 1960s and 1970s showed that despite these substantial differences in tenure patterns, ethnic minority people were much more likely than whites to be living in lower-standard and more crowded accommodation. Discrimination in both the private rented sector and the council sector was a key factor behind this development.

Comparison of the findings of the two previous surveys of ethnic minorities with those of the 1982 survey showed that whilst there was evidence of some marginal change, the dominant image was one of the continuity of these themes over time. Ethnic minority people remained in the lower status jobs in distinct parts of the economy, they still suffered substantially higher rates of unemployment than existed in the white population, and were more likely to be living in lower-standard accommodation. Not only had there not been a convergence of job patterns between white and ethnic minority people, but high and persistent unemployment affected ethnic minorities even more seriously than white people.

Since this time there have been no further purpose-built surveys of racial minorities in Britain. This report has utilised the best information on ethnic minority people that is presently available to give as broad an account as possible of the pattern of racial disadvantage at the end of the 1980s. It is important to stress again the point that we made in Chapter 1 about the nature of the LFS. The findings that we have presented almost certainly understate the extent of the disadvantage experienced by ethnic minorities. This is because the LFS fails to include those people who have little or no English, who are most likely to suffer disadvantages. This limitation is particularly serious with regard to the LFS findings for the Bangladeshi and Chinese populations.

In the past, some have tried to explain the existence of widespread racial disadvantage as a consequence of the unfamiliarity of immigrants with the housing and labour markets, the education system, and other institutions of the society into which they have come. According to this argument, as an increasing proportion of ethnic minority people are born and educated in Britain, the passage of time will by itself begin to erode these disadvantages. The findings of previous research concerning the strong persistence of inequality undermined such arguments. On the evidence of what has gone before, we may have expected to find strong elements of continuity in the patterns of racial disadvantage at the end of the 1980s with earlier periods. But the 1980s is generally accepted to have been a decade of substantial

149

political and social change, which affected people in differing ways in most sections of society.

Successive governments reversed the post-war trend and followed policies broadly aimed at reducing the size and influence of the public sector, and enhancing individual responsibility and enterprise. A number of the wider developments in British society over the past decade have particular significance for the position of the ethnic minority population. For example, the changes in the structure of employment resulting in a sharp contraction in the number of jobs in manufacturing and a simultaneous expansion in employment in the private services sector. Governments have encouraged the growth of owner-occupation in the population at large and especially in the lower socio-economic groups. They have introduced major reforms in local government and the National Health Service, both traditionally employers of large proportions of the ethnic minority workforce. The Education Reform Act 1988 makes provision for maintained schools to opt out of local education authority control. This has fuelled some calls for separate schools within the state system by some religious groups. These are just some of the many wider developments in British society over the 1980s which have major implications for the circumstances of the ethnic minority populations. Of course, the data available in the LFS do not permit us to measure directly the effects of such wider developments. However, the findings presented in this study do suggest a number of substantial changes from the pattern shown by earlier studies, along with equally strong evidence of elements of continuity. These developments are summarised in the following themes.

Divergence between different ethnic minority groups
Previous studies have acknowledged the diversity between different groups within the ethnic minority population. The report of the 1974 survey of ethnic minorities stated that the findings 'consistently show up not only the contrast between Asians and West Indians, but also the great diversity of origin, language, religion and culture among the Asians'.[1] One thing that immigrants had in common was that they all took the radical decision to leave their homes and try to make a better life for themselves and their families in a new country. All the research to date has shown another common element between different ethnic minority groups. They were all largely confined to a substantially poorer set of circumstances as compared to the white population, and these patterns remained for them and their children for decades after the initial immigration. In the *Black and White Britain* report, results were often given for Afro-Caribbeans, and all the South Asian groups taken together, which showed both groups were

generally in a poorer position compared to the white population. Thus, whilst differing degrees of disadvantage were recognised, the overall impression was one of contrast between the circumstances of whites and more poorly-off 'blacks'. The latest findings from the LFS show that a simple comparison between whites and all ethnic minorities (taken together) is increasingly likely to hide as much as it tells us.

Within the ethnic minority population there is an increasing disparity between the circumstances of specific groups. The findings suggest that the South Asian population contains both the most and the least successful of the ethnic minority groups that we have studied. At one extreme we have the African Asian and Indian populations. These groups have higher proportions of well-qualified people, have attained comparable (or better) job levels to whites, and have unemployment rates closest to those found among the white population. At the opposite end of the spectrum there are the Pakistanis and the Bangladeshis. They retain the largest proportion, even among young people, with no formal qualifications of any ethnic groups. They have substantially lower job levels than people of other origins, and consistently suffer the highest rates of unemployment.

The Afro-Caribbean population tend to fall into a position which is somewhere in between these two extremes. The Chinese appear to be in a similar position to the African Asians and the Indians. They too are highly qualified and on average appear to have better jobs than the whites. Their unemployment rates tend to be lower than those found among the white population. The other ethnic group not to have been included in earlier studies, the Africans, are more varied. In terms of family structure and household characteristics, there are broad areas of similarity with the Afro-Caribbean population. For example, these are the two groups with the highest proportion of female heads of household and female lone parent family units. In terms of education, though, there are substantial differences between these two groups. Young African people are substantially more likely to stay on in post compulsory education, and Africans are generally better qualified than whites, as well as Afro-Caribbeans. African men have better job levels than Afro-Caribbeans (although not as good as white men), although the unemployment rates in the two populations are similar.

These findings, which will be discussed in greater detail below, underline the growing differences between the position of different ethnic minorities in Britain. The essential diversity of the different ethnic groups is perhaps overcoming the common role in which immigrants were cast by British society.

Progress of particular minority ethnic groups
Three minority ethnic groups in particular – African Asians, and those originating from India and China – appear on a number of measures from the LFS to be occupying a similar position in the labour market.

African Asian, Indian and Chinese men are more likely to be highly qualified than are white men. This is particularly the case among those aged 16-24, and especially among African Asians. The high proportion (relative to whites) of these groups who are staying in full-time education is now reflected in measures of educational attainment. Also, this high level of qualification now appears to be having some effect in the job market. The proportion of male employees from each of the African Asian, Indian, and Chinese groups who are in the top job level category (professional, manager or employer) is now equal to or greater than the proportion of white men. This is not such a new phenomenon in the case of African Asians. Even in 1982, *Black and White Britain* found that there was a higher proportion of African Asian men in the top job category than of white men. However, during the 1980s people of Indian origin substantially increased their representation in the higher levels of the job market. Whilst earlier studies did not cover people of Chinese origin, LFS data from the mid-1980s show that they had a high proportion of male employees in the better jobs then. Evidence from the LFS that the Chinese are a relatively well-placed group in the labour market contrasts sharply with that from the SCPR survey in Scotland, which found the Chinese to be one of the most deprived groups.

This is a major change from earlier studies which generally found that even well-qualified people from ethnic minority groups were more often confined to lower job levels than similarly qualified whites. This increase in the proportion of certain ethnic minority groups in the top categories of job results from an increase in the numbers of well-qualified men entering professional jobs like accountancy and medicine, although sample sizes prevent us from analysing the actual types of jobs in more detail. White men in the top category are more likely to be managers in large establishments than in professional jobs. Of those men with higher qualifications (A level or above), the African Asians, Indians and Chinese are substantially more likely to be in professional jobs than white men. The importance of educational qualifications in this development is also suggested by the fact that among men of lower or no qualifications, the disparity between the job levels of whites and even the more successful ethnic minority groups still persists.

Just as the African Asian, Indian and Chinese groups appear to be making progress in terms of education and employment, when we examine national unemployment rates these same groups have rates that are nearer to the white rate than any other minority group. The Chinese tend to have the lowest unemployment rates of all ethnic groups (including the whites). The African Asians have slightly higher rates, and the Indians higher again. This general pattern persists within age groups, job levels, and qualification levels, and whether or not the highest qualification was gained in Britain.

So from the evidence available in the LFS, it appears that some ethnic minority groups have made progress overall in the labour market during the 1980s in comparison both with whites and with other minority groups. There are a number of possible explanations for this. The first involves general trends in the pattern of employment. As we mentioned above, the 1980s saw a general shift in employment away from manufacturing and towards the service sector. It does appear that this shift has been accompanied by an upward movement in average job levels. Earlier studies found that the disparity between the job levels of white and ethnic minority employees was greatest in manufacturing industry, so we should expect the relative decline of manufacturing to have a stronger effect upon the average job levels of ethnic minorities. But the changes in the distribution of job levels that we have seen cannot be explained with reference to such structural factors alone, since some ethnic groups have progressed much more than others. It may be that the expansion in the professional service sector during the 1980s provided a window of opportunity for those members of certain ethnic minority groups who hold higher qualifications.

Another possible explanation is the development of business among the South Asian and Chinese populations, who have the highest proportions of self-employed of all ethnic groups. The development of business networks within certain ethnic minority communities may act as a buffer to unemployment, and provide opportunities for upward mobility that do not exist in the wider job market. One argument put forward in the past has been that the high incidence of self-employment among South Asians in particular reflects a strategy to avoid competition with whites in a restricted labour market. Unfortunately, the information available from the LFS does not allow us to analyse in more detail the development of ethnic minority businesses. It is not possible to identify the ethnic group of business-owners or show family workers separately. However, the fact is that a large part of the increase in the proportion of certain groups in the top job category is accounted for by highly-qualified professional workers. This may well suggest that people from some ethnic minority groups are increasingly competing, successfully, in the higher reaches of the job market.

A third factor underlying the apparent improvement in the employment prospects of some ethnic minority groups is the demographic trends of the late 1980s. The changing age structure of the population combined with the expansion of demand in the British economy to produce labour shortages, particularly in the South East of England. This may have provided new impetus for employers to try actively to recruit members of ethnic minority groups in the face of a shrinking labour supply. It is not possible to measure the effect of such factors at a national level, and equally impossible to measure the probable reverse trend once the economy entered into recession again.

Continuing disadvantage of some ethnic groups
The apparent progress of some specific ethnic minority groups contrasts with the continued disadvantage of others. The Afro-Caribbeans and particularly the Pakistanis and Bangladeshis are consistently in lower level jobs and suffer from higher unemployment rates than the white population. Pakistanis and Bangladeshis stand out as the two groups consistently in poorer circumstances than all others.

Both Pakistani and Bangladeshi young people are more likely than whites to stay in full-time education after age 16. However, in terms of overall educational attainment they still lag far behind. The Pakistanis and Bangladeshis are by some way the least likely groups to hold formal qualifications. This is particularly true for women, of whom high proportions have never received any formal education at all. Despite our finding that in the 16-24 age group there was much less disparity between the levels of qualification of different ethnic groups, the Pakistani and Bangladeshi population still remained substantially behind other groups. This is not a surprising finding in that of all the groups studied, the Pakistanis and Bangladeshis are relatively likely to have less English.

This lower level of qualification manifests itself in lower job levels in the labour market. But even within qualification levels, male employees from these two groups have an inferior distribution of jobs compared with other ethnic groups. Overall, the proportion of Pakistani and Bangladeshi male employees in the top job category has barely changed since 1982. At the same time, these two groups retain high proportions of employees in the semi-skilled and unskilled categories. The most striking example of this is the Bangladeshi group. At the end of a decade in which there has been a general contraction of lower level manual jobs, there is still the same 70 per cent of male Bangladeshi employees in semi-skilled and unskilled manual work as there was in 1982.

It is hardly surprising then that Pakistani and Bangladeshi workers are still more vulnerable than workers of other ethnic origins to unemployment. But as with previous research, job levels only explain a part of this disparity.

Even within job levels, Pakistani and Bangladeshi workers have substantially higher unemployment rates than other groups. This remains the case if we control for age group, qualification, or region of residence. In some cases, controlling for such factors makes the differences even greater.

The case of Afro-Caribbean people is more complex. They tend to be in a position which falls somewhere between those of the whites, African Asians, Indians and Chinese on the one hand, and the Pakistanis and Bangladeshis on the other. The Afro-Caribbean population is the longest-established of all the major post-1945 settlement groups included in this study. Their continuing position of overall disadvantage compared to the white population, and to groups within the more recently-arrived South Asian population, is therefore particularly striking.

In terms of education, Afro-Caribbean men and women are both more likely than their white counterparts to stay on in full-time education after age 16. Other studies, including the YCS, suggest that Afro-Caribbeans are more inclined than people from other ethnic groups towards vocational qualifications. The LFS shows that on a broad level, Afro-Caribbean men have comparable school-level qualifications to white men, but fewer of them have higher qualifications. In contrast, Afro-Caribbean women tend to be better-qualified than women of other ethnic origins. In the job market, despite the fact that Afro-Caribbean men have more than doubled the proportion of their employees in the top job category, they still have one of the lowest proportions in this group. The reduction of lower level manual jobs has been accompanied by an expansion of Afro-Caribbean employment in the 'other non-manual' category. They retain a high proportion of skilled manual workers. Over half of Afro-Caribbean male employees qualified to A level or higher are working in manual jobs. Unemployment rates among Afro-Caribbeans are substantially higher than those found among the white population, though not as high as among the Pakistani and Bangladeshi populations.

A number of factors could lie behind the continued disadvantage of certain ethnic minority groups. Research has shown that the level of racial discrimination was the same in the mid-1980s as it was during the mid-1970s.[2] But given the apparent progress of some ethnic minority groups, it is not possible to attribute racial disadvantage *purely* to discrimination. Previous research found that racial discrimination was experienced equally by all ethnic minority groups. If we accept this, to explain the disadvantage of specific ethnic groups in terms of discrimination *alone* begs the question as to why this same effect is apparently not as extensive in other ethnic minority groups. If we are to argue that racial discrimination is the key factor behind racial disadvantage, we must accept one of two propositions. First, that different ethnic groups now face different levels of racial discrimination. This seems highly unlikely given the findings of previous research, and the fact that both the most and least successful groups in the ethnic minority population have a similar skin colour. A second, and more likely, proposition is that some groups are better placed to develop ways of overcoming the constraints set by discrimination.

The fact that Pakistanis and Bangladeshis are relatively recently-arrived populations may explain at least a part of their relative disadvantage. However, relatively high proportions of the African Asian and Chinese populations also arrived from 1970 onwards, and these are two of the better-off groups. The Afro-Caribbeans remain in a substantially poorer position overall compared to whites, despite being one of the longest-established of the ethnic minorities in Britain. So length of residence in this country cannot explain by itself the relative positions of different groups. It is particularly difficult to explain the disparity between groups who share a similar skin colour. One possible explanation concerns the history and traditions of different groups prior to migration. The Bangladeshis tended to come to Britain to escape the poverty in their home country, bringing with them relatively little in terms of capital and educational qualifications. African Asians, on the other hand, came to Britain to flee political persecution in East Africa. Prior to this, they had formed a highly successful business community, and many were able to bring with them skills, qualifications and even capital to help them in their new country. It is hardly surprising therefore, that a group like the African Asians appears to be defeating the constraints imposed by discrimination and disadvantage more quickly than other ethnic minorities. In the previous section, we mentioned self-employment as a possible channel of upward mobility and buffer against unemployment for some South Asian groups. But this leaves unanswered the question of why this effect does not occur to the same extent in the Pakistani and Bangladeshi communities.

It is clear that general circumstances have changed little for people of Afro-Caribbean, Pakistani and Bangladeshi origin since 1982. They remain concentrated in lower job levels, and are subject to much higher rates of unemployment than other ethnic groups. More detailed research is required to explain this continued relative disadvantage.

Disparity within ethnic groups
As we have said, there is clear evidence that overall, some ethnic minority groups have substantially improved their position in the labour market since

1982. But we should beware of assuming from this that ethnic minorities as a whole, or that all members of those specific groups, are in substantially better circumstances. Whilst the divergence between specific ethnic groups has been increasing, there remains considerable disparity within ethnic groups. For example, there are relatively high proportions of Indian and Chinese male employees in the top job category (professional, manager, employer), but also a high proportion in semi-skilled and unskilled manual work. We have already referred to the Home Affairs Select Committee report of 1984-85 which drew attention to the narrow range of job opportunities for Chinese people, who tend to enter either the catering trade or the professions. But many people are too qualified for most catering jobs but not appropriately qualified to be in professional work. African Asians and Indians, whilst having lower unemployment rates than most other minority populations, still have higher rates than the white population. Other research has found a polarisation developing within certain ethnic groups. Robinson has suggested a growing gulf within the Indian population between an expanding middle class, and manual classes who are much more vulnerable to unemployment.[3]

During the 1980s, the real earnings of those in employment have risen constantly over the decade. Evidence from the New Earnings Survey has shown that this growth in real earnings has been substantially greater in some occupations than others. For example, during the period 1979-86, real earnings in the professional management group rose by 29 per cent compared to 3 per cent in construction and mining.[4] An increase in the size of occupational groups at the top end of the distribution will have the effect of widening the earnings distribution within certain groups. As mentioned in chapter 4, detailed information about earnings differentials both between and within ethnic groups is not presently available. Until it is, we are restricted to making suggestions based on knowledge about what has happened to job levels in the various minority groups. The increased proportions of male employees in the top category, particularly for those groups who retain a relatively large proportion in semi-skilled and unskilled manual work, suggest that disparity in terms of earnings has increased within, as well as between ethnic groups.

One important element of disparity within ethnic groups is the comparative circumstances of men and women. For example, a notable feature of our findings about the Afro-Caribbean population is the sharp contrast between the circumstances of Afro-Caribbean women when compared to other ethnic groups, and those of Afro-Caribbean men. This reflects the important economic role traditionally played by Afro-Caribbean women. They exhibit higher economic activity rates than women of other ethnic groups, whether or not they have dependent children. The Afro-Caribbean population has the highest proportion of households headed by a women, and the highest proportion of female lone parent families. Afro-Caribbean women employees have similar job levels to those of white women, whereas Afro-Caribbean men remain in substantially lower jobs than those of white men. Afro-Caribbean women have high rates of trade union membership compared to women of other ethnic origins. Women from this group tend to have lower unemployment rates than men, and are less likely to be out of work for more than a year (although this is also true of women in other ethnic groups when compared with men).

The position of women in the South Asian population shows strong elements of continuity with past research. Bangladeshi and Pakistani women, who are nearly all Muslims, have very low rates of economic activity; very high proportions do not work outside the home. Also, high proportions have no formal qualifications: many never had any schooling at all. The 1986 Home Affairs Committee report on the Bangladeshi population in Britain noted how many of the problems experienced by people from this ethnic group affected women in particular.[5] African Asian and Indian women have economic activity rates and qualification levels nearer to those of white women, and there is far less difference between the positions of men and women overall within these ethnic groups.

This report has shown elements of both change and continuity in the circumstances of Britain's ethnic minorities. The varied findings are open to alternative interpretations. Optimists could highlight the growing number of men from the ethnic minorities who have gained entry to the higher job levels, the continued evidence of the drive to educational attainment (particularly apparent now in the younger age groups), and the narrowing of the racial disparity in unemployment rates since the mid-1980s. They might argue from these facts that there has been a real improvement in equality of opportunity in British society, and that the effects of racial discrimination are diminishing. Pessimists, on the other hand, could point out that after over three decades of living in Britain, large proportions of people belonging to ethnic minorities remain economically vulnerable, concentrated in lower job levels and subject to higher rates of unemployment than the white population, even among the more successful minority groups, and even within qualification levels. They might further argue that much of the apparent progress of certain groups reflects the economic cycle rather than a change towards a more open society. As the economy moves back into long-term recession during the 1990s they might argue that racial differences in unemployment rates are widening once again, and that the apparent improvements in the prospects of those in work are looking increasingly precarious.

Such selective and over-simplified conclusions should not be drawn from this study. It has revealed a more complex pattern than previous research: there are various degrees of disparity within and between racial groups that can no longer be adequately summarised by a simple contrast between relatively well-off 'whites' and poorly-off 'blacks' (who consist of all the diverse ethnic minorities grouped together). However, the nature of the LFS, a general purpose survey not designed with ethnic minorities in mind, prevents a more refined understanding and explanation of these changes. This survey does not allow a more detailed analysis of occupations here grouped into broad categories; nor can the condition of ethnic minorities be analysed in relation to the characteristics of the local areas where they live and work. Most crucially, the LFS provides no information about ethnic differences in income and earnings. This report has shown that important and complex changes in the position of ethnic minorities are taking place. The challenge for future research is to provide a clearer understanding of what these changes are, and why they are happening.

Notes

1. David J. Smith, *The Facts of Racial Disadvantage*, PEP, 1976, p.180.
2. C. Brown and P. Gay, *Racial Discrimination: 17 Years After the Act*, PSI, 1986.
3. V. Robinson, 'The new Indian middle class in Britain', *Ethnic and Racial Studies*, 11.4, 1988.
4. M. Adams, R. Maybury and W. Smith, 'Trends in the distribution of earnings 1973-1986', *Employment Gazette*, 96.2, 1988.
5. House of Commons, First Report from the Home Affairs Committee, Session 1967-87, *Bangladeshis in Britain*.

Appendix 1

The balance of the sample

Black and White Britain covered people of Afro-Caribbean (West Indian), Indian, Pakistani, Bangladeshi, and African Asian origin. The table below uses LFS-based (see table 2.1) estimates of the growth of the various ethnic minority populations to gross up the PSI 1982 estimates to 1988-90, so that the sample balance between different ethnic groups can be compared with the balance between the same groups in the 1988-90 LFS.

Balance of ethnic groups compared between PSI survey of 1982 and LFS of 1988-90

	PSI Survey 1982 Column %	Change 1981-88/90 % change	PSI Survey Grossed to 1988-90 Column %	LFS 1988-90 Column %
Afro-Caribbean	33	-5	25	26
African Asian	13	+40	15	14
Indian	27	+5	23	30
Pakistani	20	+58	25	24
Bangladeshi	7	+110	12	6
Total	100		100	100

These findings give only a rough indication of the comparison between the balance of ethnic groups in the two samples; one reason for this is that the estimate of population growth for African Asians does not relate to exactly the same group as the one identified either in the 1982 PSI survey or in the LFS analysis. On the whole there is a fair degree of consistency between the 1982 figures updated for population growth and the 1988-90 LFS figures, but there are two important discrepancies. First, there is a considerably higher proportion of Indians in the LFS than in the updated PSI figures. Second, the 1982 survey contained twice the proportion of Bangladeshis as the LFS. This supports the idea that the LFS under-estimates the more recently-arrived immigrant populations having relatively few English speakers. This is a major limitation which should always be remembered when interpreting the LFS results.

Appendix 2

Definition of ethnic groups

White	White, white-mixed, white-other
Afro-Caribbean	West Indian/Guyanese, West Indian/Guyanese-white mixed, West Indian/Guyanese-other
African Asian	See Chapter 1
Indian	Indian, Indian-white mixed, Indian-other
Pakistani	Pakistani, Pakistani-white mixed, Pakistani-other
Bangladeshi	Bangladeshi, Bangladeshi-white mixed, Bangladeshi-other
Chinese	Chinese, Chinese-other
African	African, African-white mixed, African-West Indian mixed, African-Asian mixed, African-other
Other/Mixed	Other, Arab, Mixed, other Asian-white mixed, Asian mixture, miscellaneous partly coloured, miscellaneous coloured, other Asian, insufficient information.
All ethnic minorities	All groups except white

Appendix 3

Definition of highest qualification

Degree or equivalent   Higher degree, first degree, other degree-level qualification

Higher education below degree level   BTEC, SCOTBTEC, BEC, SCOTBEC, TEC, SCOTEC, SCOTVEC (higher), HNC, HND, teaching qualification at secondary level, teaching qualification at primary level, nursing qualification

GCE A level or equivalent   BTEC, SCOTBTEC, BEC, SCOTBEC, TEC, SCOTEC, SCOTVEC (national general) ONC, OND, City and Guilds, A level or equivalent, SLC (higher), SCE (higher), SUPE (higher), Certificate of 6th year studies, Trade Apprenticeship

GCE O level or equivalent   O level or equivalent including CSE grade 1, SLC (lower), SCE (ordinary), SUPE (lower or ordinary)

CSE (other than grade 1)   as written

Any other professional or vocational qualification   as written

No qualification   as written

Appendix 4

Definition of socio-economic groups

1. Employers and managers (large establishments)
2. Employers and managers (small establishments)
3. Professional workers (self-employed)
4. Professional workers (employed)
5. Intermediate non-manual workers
6. Junior non-manual workers
7. Personal Service workers
8. Foreman and Supervisor - Manual
9. Skilled Manual workers
10. Semi-Skilled Manual workers
11. Unskilled Manual workers
12. Own Account Workers
13. Farmers - Employers and Managers
14. Farmers - Own Account
15. Agricultural workers
16. Members of Armed Services

For the analysis the above SEG categories were grouped as follows.

Job level	SEG codes
Professional, Employer, Manager	1, 2, 3, 4, 13
Other Non-Manual	5, 6
Skilled Manual & Foreman	8, 9, 12, 14
Semi-Skilled Manual	7, 10, 15
Unskilled Manual	11

NB this is based on the 1980 Classification of Occupations

Appendix 5

Unweighted base numbers for three years, 1988-90

Absolute numbers

	All origins	White	Total ethnic minority	Afro-Caribbean	African Asian	Indian	Paki-stani	Bangla-deshi	Chinese	African	Other Mixed
All											
All persons	458201	431858	21185	4138	2166	4703	3828	854	1104	1249	3143
All working age	276653	261026	12737	2756	1400	2948	1927	418	763	785	1740
Age 16-24	58421	54203	3365	762	305	754	571	144	166	185	478
Age 25-44	130836	123126	6399	1162	878	1346	948	170	454	459	982
Age 45-59/64	87396	83697	2973	832	217	848	408	104	143	141	280
All employees	176658	169148	6145	1653	792	1384	544	125	316	402	929
All self-employed	26928	25498	1215	150	184	365	178	32	134	35	137
All unemployed	16873	15575	1145	317	96	241	217	51	35	69	119
All households	181771	174255	6009	1614	521	1298	771	171	331	458	845
All family units	198610	189297	7224	1800	631	1636	944	214	427	548	1024
Men											
All	222332	209089	10702	1986	1110	2365	2021	451	568	601	1600
All working age	142229	134292	6429	1316	713	1499	1008	221	386	393	893
Age 16-24	29064	26956	1668	356	147	369	299	71	89	92	245
Age 25-44	64141	60431	3039	512	442	645	440	79	209	217	495
Age 45-64	49024	46905	1722	448	124	485	269	71	88	84	153
All employees	93660	89559	3372	762	422	768	436	101	161	209	513
All unemployed	9707	8932	690	165	48	145	166	40	27	39	60
Women											
All	235869	222769	10483	2152	1056	2338	1807	403	536	648	1543
All working age	134424	126734	6308	1440	687	1449	919	197	377	392	847
Age 16-24	29357	27247	1697	406	158	385	272	73	77	93	233
Age 25-44	66695	62695	3360	650	436	701	508	91	245	242	487
Age 45-59	38372	36792	1251	384	93	363	139	33	55	57	127
All employees	82998	79589	2773	891	370	616	108	24	155	193	416
All unemployed	7166	6643	455	152	48	96	51	11	8	30	59

Source: 1988, 1989, 1990 Labour Force Surveys (GB)